HELLO.

MY NAME IS:

_____

MY BIRTHDAY IS ON:

_____

I WAS BORN IN:

_____

MY FAMILY MEMBERS ARE:

_____

_____

_____

_____

THIS IS WHAT I LOOK LIKE:

I LIVE IN:

_____

AND THIS IS THE
GREAT BIG ME EXPERIMENT

To ME. And to YOU, too. —AB
To Adrian. —HB

An imprint of Macmillan Children's Publishing Group, LLC
120 Broadway, New York, NY 10271 • OddDot.com • mackids.com

WRITER Alli Brydon
ILLUSTRATOR Harry Briggs
DESIGNER Tae Won Yu
EDITOR Justin Krasner

Library of Congress Control Number: 2022949549

Our books are available at special discounts when purchased in bulk for premiums and
sales promotions as well as for fund-raising or educational use. Special editions or
book excerpts also can be created to specification. For details, contact the Macmillan
Corporate and Premium Sales Department at (800) 221-7945 ext. 5442, or send an email to
MacmillanSpecialMarkets@macmillan.com.

First edition, 2023
Printed in China by 1010 Printing International Limited, Kwun Tong, Hong Kong

ISBN 978-1-250-82807-1
1 3 5 7 9 10 8 6 4 2

Joyful Books for Curious Minds

THE GREAT BIG ME

75 ACTIVITIES TO DISCOVER ALL ABOUT YOU

EXPERIMENT

ALLI BRYDON

ILLUSTRATED BY HARRY BRIGGS

Odd Dot • New York

CONTENTS

WELCOME TO THE GREAT BIG ME EXPERIMENT!

Welcome to this book, *The Great Big ME Experiment*. Above all, this book is about YOU. Wait—how did all your deep, dark secrets get found out, written down, and then published in this book?! Do not panic: Your secrets have *not* been discovered. Yet.

With this book, you will uncover the great secrets about yourself, all by yourself. No need to show anyone. No need to tell anyone…unless you want to.

This book is filled with experiments—some silly, some serious, some sloppy—to help you discover the very *you*-ness of YOU. But these experiments are not like the ones you've done in science class, with beakers, mixtures, and explosive stuff. That is, unless your innermost self is rather explosive (which it probably is)! This is a science class of one: for numero uno, the big cheese, the CEO of your life…YOU! It's also gym class, a guidance counselor session, a walk through the cafeteria, and a field trip into the wild.

Think you already know yourself, inside and out? Um, have you done "The Cilantro Taste Test"? Have you ever tried to describe your own farts? Have you ever assigned colors to your feelings? Do you know if you're an introvert or an extrovert…or even what either of those things mean?! You're a really smart kid, but you probably don't know the half of all the unique and incredible things about YOU. But you will!

The Great Big ME Experiment is broken up into four parts, all about: your body, your feelings, your mind, and your humanity. Each part dives deep into that topic to show you the remarkable, surprising, beautiful, and messy stuff inside us all. These experiments will test you, teach you, make you giggle, and make you go "Whaaaa?!" They will inspire wonder, because you are quite a wonderful thing.

So, grab some trusty sneakers, safety goggles, crampons and a carabiner, provisions for a week, a wet suit, a box of tissues, a psychic squirrel, and a full set of body armor. Just kidding! All you need is this book, a pen and notebook, some household items, and yourself (and maybe that box of tissues to catch your boogers).

Get ready to experiment on…YOU!

HAVE YOU EVER HEARD OF THE SCIENTIFIC METHOD?

It's the way you conduct an experiment, from start to finish. Scientists always start with a BIG QUESTION. In this case, your big question is: "Who am I?" All the activities in this book will help you find the answer to that question.

PART 1

MY ONE-AND-ONLY BOD

Welcome to your very own outrageous, bodacious body! This part is all about your amazing body and testing it (safely!) to its limits. You might think you know your body inside and out. Think again! You're about to find out some incredible things about YOU that you never knew before.

As you discover what your body can do, remember that you are a superstar just the way you are. Nothing is "normal" or "abnormal" here. All bodies are different—it's one thing that makes the world so cool. Imagine if we were all exactly the same, like robots or clones. Boring!

So, some of these experiments might look different for you. Skip any that make you feel uncomfortable. And if you have any food allergies, please think twice about what you put in your mouth, aight?

Now, prepare to get WOW-ed, grossed out, tickled pink (literally), and totally mindful about your one-and-only bod!

FAB FINGERPRINTS

Fingerprints are exactly what they sound like: the print pattern made by your fingertips. There are eight common types of human fingerprint patterns:

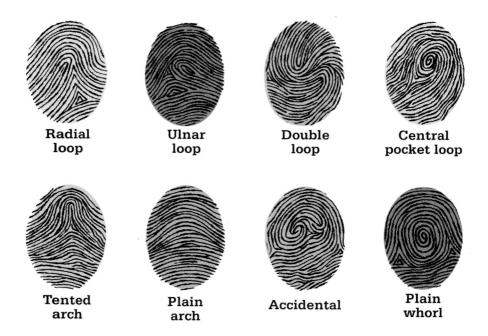

| Radial loop | Ulnar loop | Double loop | Central pocket loop |
| Tented arch | Plain arch | Accidental | Plain whorl |

Even though all humans have ten unique fingerprints that fall into the eight main types above, no two people have the exact same one—not even twins. You are a wonderful, unique design from your head to the very tips of your fingers. It's true!

Your fingerprints do not change at all throughout your lifetime. Even if you burn your fingertips, the new skin will grow back in the exact same pattern as before! That's why fingerprints can be used as a way of identifying people.

WHAT YOU'LL NEED

- Dark ink pad or marker
- Your fingers (don't forget these!)

WHAT YOU'LL DO

1. Make sure your fingers are clean and dry.

2. Place the ink pad on a flat surface.

3. Get your fingertips inky by placing each one tip down onto the ink (or coloring them with your marker). Roll your fingertip around in the ink to make sure it's fully covered.

4. Press your fingertips into the boxes below, one at a time, to make your marks.

5. Compare them to the print patterns above. What type of fingerprints do you have?

RIGHT HAND

THUMB	POINTER	MIDDLE	RING	PINKIE

LEFT HAND

PINKIE	RING	MIDDLE	POINTER	THUMB

Now go wash those fingertips!

FART SOMMELIER

Have you ever heard the word *sommelier* (pronounced som-MELL-ee-ay)? It's just a fancy way to say "wine expert." Sommeliers use their taste buds and noses to sniff a whiff and describe the smell to non-wine experts. They say things like:

> THIS TOASTY VINTAGE HAS HINTS OF **BLUE-NESS** ON THE FRONT END, BALANCED WITH **CAT PEE** AND A **CHEWY FINISH.**

> **CHUNKY** AND **SWEET**, BUT NOT **SYRUPY**, WITH OODLES OF FRESH **SUMMER LAVENDER** ON THE END NOTES.

Expert-sounding right? Kinda gross-sounding, too. Well, you can't drink wine yet, but you *can* become an expert on...your own FARTS!

Everybody farts: You (don't even try saying you don't!). Your sister. Your best friend. Definitely your dad. Maybe your mom. Your teacher. Your grandma and grandpa (okay, stop thinking about your grandpa's farts). Even the coolest kid at school farts. Everyone passes gas about twenty times a day. So, if someone tries to pass it off like they never fart, they're bluffing. Your farts come from deep inside your gut. They are a part of you...until they're floating in the air behind you.

Next time you pass gas, try describing what you smell. You can become a sommelier, or expert, on your own farts with this handy chart of adjectives and nouns:

ADJECTIVES

RANCID   FRUITY   EFFERVESCENT   SPICY
WHIFFY   BUTTERY   SWEET   AROMATIC
HUGE   MALODOROUS   STRONG   CHUNKY

NOUNS

CABBAGE   HOT DOG   CHEESE   TACO   GARLIC   DIRT
SUNSHINE   BEAN   ONION   SOUR APPLE   BROCCOLI

This toot is deliciously _____ and _____
[adjective]   [adjective]

on the palate, with _____ notes, and finishing
                          [adjective]

off with a _____ and _____ flavor-bomb.
              [noun]   [noun]

When you smell and describe your farts, try to remember what you ate last. Can you detect that in your fart's *odeur*? Are there certain foods that make you gassier? Are there certain foods that make your farts smellier? What are they? Create a Fart Diary to keep track of your toots!

OH, B.O.!

Body odor, also affectionately known as B.O., is a smelly rite of passage. During puberty, which happens anytime between the ages of eight and fourteen, the smell of your sweat goes from pretty to pretty stinky. Blame those hormones!

But even if you haven't hit puberty yet, you smell. (What? Don't scowl, it's a scientific fact!) Why don't you take a whiff of yourself, and note:

Where is your body smelly?

_____

What do you smell like after you go outside to play?

_____

Does your body smell differently after you eat certain foods?

_____

How does your body smell after exercise?

_____

How does your body smell after you sit on the couch, eat junk food, and watch TV all day?

_____

What do you smell like after you stay inside all day?

_____

TELL YOUR SMELL

Speaking of the smelly stuff, did you know that each person has their very own scent? Your scent is sublimely, uniquely yours, just like your fingerprint. Can you tell your smell?

WHAT YOU'LL NEED

- Three identical, clean pillowcases

WHAT YOU'LL DO

1. Get your three identical, clean pillowcases out. They should be the same size and color, so you can't tell which is which just by looking at them.

2. Place one of the pillowcases on your pillow and sleep on it. Try not to drool!

3. When you wake up, take off the pillowcase you slept on and mix it up with the ones you didn't.

4. Sniff all three pillowcases. Can you find the one you slept on overnight? Can anyone else tell which pillowcase you slept on?

5. Describe your scent here.

DISSECT A BOOGER

Okay, so while we're talking sniffers…how many golden nuggets are up your nostrils?

Your nose's #1 job is to smell, but do you know what its #2 job is? Making boogers! Boogers are basically hardened snot, or mucus. Sticky mucus lines your nostrils and nasal sinuses. I'm sure you already know what it looks like, but go ahead and blow your nose into a tissue and then have a peek.

MUCUS
IS VERY IMPORTANT FOR THREE REASONS:

1. It keeps your nostrils and sinuses moist, happy, and working well.

2. It protects the very delicate lining of your nostrils and sinuses from irritation.

3. It traps dust, dirt, and other junk before you can inhale them into your body.

Boogers form when this sticky mucus gets dried up by air. Okay, so you're not supposed to stick your finger up your nose to pick your boogers (so rude). BUT! If one happens to "fall" out of your nose, place it on a tissue to do this experiment. We're going to examine a booger.

WHAT YOU'LL NEED

- Chunky piece of gold from your nostril (aka a booger)
- Tissue
- Pair of tweezers (make sure you clean them very well with soap and water after this experiment is over)
- Magnifying glass
- Toothpick

WHAT YOU'LL DO

1. Place your booger very carefully on a tissue that's been laid out flat on a table.

2. Using the tweezers, pick up your booger and hold it up to the light. What color is it? Is it many colors? Is it see-through or opaque? Is it wet or dry?

3. Keep holding the booger with the tweezers, and now take a magnifying glass to it. What does it look like up close? Can you see many particles in it?

4. Now place the booger back on the tissue. Using the toothpick, poke at your booger and notice how it feels. Is it sticky? Is it really hard? Does it come apart or stay together?

5. Now place the booger in your mouth—EWW!!!!! Just kidding, that's gross. Don't do that! You can throw it in the garbage now.

6. Make notes about all the things you've discovered about your boogers.

What's really in a booger? Dried mucus mixed with bits of dust, pollen, bacteria, and other mystery stuff!

AHEM! Go and wash your hands now, thankyouverymuch!

HOT OR COLD?

Do you like warm, sunny beaches or magical, snowy mountains? Are you always freezing or always sweating? Are you a "hot" person or a "cold" person? Maybe you are both!

EASY FREEZY

WHAT YOU'LL NEED

- 2 medium-sized bowls
- Ice cubes
- Water
- Timer or stopwatch

WHAT YOU'LL DO

1. Fill one bowl with ice cubes and the other bowl with cold water.

2. Place two ice cubes in the bowl with water. Leave it for a minute so the water gets cold.

3. Stick your hand in the ice water and start your timer.

4. Every thirty seconds add another ice cube until you've used up all your ice cubes.

5. Stop the timer when you can't take any more cold!

How long did you keep your hand in the ice water?

_____
Record your time here

Let your hand warm up for 5 minutes, then try the experiment again. Can you keep your hand in the ice water for longer this time?

_____
Record your time here

WELCOME TO SWEATSVILLE

WHAT YOU'LL NEED

- Lots of clothing: long-sleeve shirts, sweaters, coats, thermal bottoms, jeans, ski pants, socks, gloves, hats—grab 'em all!
- Heater or radiator
- Timer or stopwatch

WHAT YOU'LL DO

1. Put as much clothing on your body as you possibly can. Layer up, buttercup!
2. Stand near a heater or radiator in your house. If it's summertime and there are no heaters on, that's okay. You want to test your tolerance for heat, so a hot day is as good as a toasty radiator.
3. Start your timer or stopwatch.
4. Stop the timer when you start sweating. Go ahead and pat your forehead, Sweaty Betty.

How long before you felt yourself start to sweat?

Record your time here

Take off the extra clothing and cool down. Then try the experiment again. Can you stand the heat for longer this time?

Record your time here

So...are you a "hot" person or a "cold" person?

SEE IN 2D!

With both your eyes open, you have 3D vision, which means you can see all three dimensions: length, width, and depth. But when you close one eye, you can only see in 2D. This makes it harder to do stuff, and nearly impossible to walk without bumping into things!

Test it out—but first sit down…

WHAT YOU'LL NEED

- Two sharpened pencils that are the same length

WHAT YOU'LL DO

1. Place one pencil in your hand—either one. Hold it about arm's length away from you, and focus on the pencil's point. Alternate closing your right eye and then your left. Open both eyes again. Do you notice the difference between having both eyes open, as opposed to just one?

2. Now place one pencil in each of your hands.

3. Hold the pencils parallel, at arm's length away from your face.

4. Close your left eye and try to touch the pencils' points together. Can you do it?

5. Now close your right eye and try to touch the pencils' points together again. Can you do it this time?

6. Open both eyes and try to touch the pencils' points together. It should be really easy this time!

It's fun to play around with 2D vision! Was there anything different or interesting you noticed when looking through only one eye?

NEAR OR FAR?

How good is your eyesight? Do you really know? You could be nearsighted, which means you can see close things clearly. Or you might be farsighted, meaning you can see well from far away. Or maybe you've got 20/20 vision...lucky you!

When was the last time you had your eyes checked? Why not check 'em now!*

WHAT YOU'LL NEED

- This book
- Your eyes

WHAT YOU'LL DO

1. If you wear glasses, take them off for this experiment.

2. Flip to a page of this book with a lot of writing on it. Wait—that's pretty much every page! Okay, flip to your favorite page of the book that has a lot of writing on it.

3. Hold the book about six inches away from your face (that's about the length of three thumbs). Try to read the words. How did you do?

4. Now put a bookmark in the book and close it. Place the book standing upright on a table, turn around, and walk about ten steps away from the book. Then turn back around and look at the book. Can you read the title clearly? Can you read the subtitle clearly?

If it was more comfortable to read the book when it was up close to your face, then you're nearsighted. If you read the title and subtitle better from far away, you're farsighted. If you could do both perfectly well...then congrats—you've got amazing peepers!

*Please note: This does not replace the eye doctor at all! Go get your eyes checked out once per year, please.

HYPER FLEX TEST

You know that kid at school who shows off their super flexibility and claims they are "double-jointed"? Are YOU that kid?

There is actually no such thing as being "double-jointed." Everyone has the same number of joints, which are the points where two bones meet. But some people have extra flexibility in those joints, which is known as *hypermobility*.

Hypermobile people are able to do things like bend their fingers all the way back or put their leg behind their head. Whoa! Hypermobility allows a person to move a bone beyond its normal range without feeling the same pain that a non-hypermobile person would.

Do you think you might be extra flexible? Try out this experiment based on the Beighton Scale, which experts use to test for hypermobility. But make sure you don't push yourself too far!

WHAT YOU'LL DO

1. Can you bend your pinkie finger backward more than ninety degrees? Try this out on both pinkies.

2. Can you push your thumb down to touch your forearm? Try this out on both thumbs.

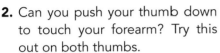

3. If you straighten your arm all the way, does your elbow extend backward? Try this on both arms.

4. If you straighten your leg all the way, does your knee extend backward? Try this on both legs.

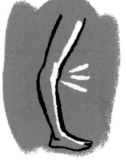

5. Can you bend forward and place your hands flat on the floor without bending your knees?

For each one you are able to do, give yourself one point. Don't forget to test both sides of your body in steps 1–4 and give yourself one point for each. If you score more than five points, you are hypermobile!

If you are hypermobile, don't worry. It's not normally harmful to your body. But be careful: Hypermobile people are more at risk of popping their joints out of place.

FINGER ON THE PULSE

Want to figure out how fast your heart is beating? It's easy. You don't even have to open up your chest and peek inside (ouch!). Count your heartbeats just by feeling your pulse.

There is a system of arteries, veins, and capillaries that carry blood throughout your body. This is called the circulatory system, and it starts and ends at your heart. It whooshes blood through your body every moment of the day. It's like a giant race track, where your blood cells are stock car racers. Each time blood pumps through your body, you can feel it by touching certain spots called *pulse points*.

Here's how you take your pulse:

WHAT YOU'LL NEED

- Your wrist
- Clock with a second hand, or a timer

WHAT YOU'LL DO

1. Hold out your left arm with your palm facing up.

2. Take the index and middle fingers of your right hand and place them onto your left wrist, just below the bottom of your thumb.

3. Press down a little bit and feel around for your pulse, which might feel like something is repeatedly jumping up and down just beneath your skin.

4. When you've found your pulse, look at your watch or set your timer for sixty seconds, and count how many pulses you feel during that time. Make sure you don't count the seconds instead of your pulses—it's easy for the brain to get confused here!

Record your resting pulse here: _____

Now try taking and recording your pulse during several activities:

When you first wake up: _____

Right before you go to bed: _____

After you run in place for a minute: _____

While watching a scary movie: _____

After getting up in front of your whole class: _____

After having a fight with a friend: _____

Before seeing someone you like: _____

After hearing your favorite song: _____

Before you eat lunch: _____

After you eat lunch: _____

How does the speed of your pulse change with each of these activities?

If you stretched out all your blood vessels and laid them flat on the ground, they would circle Earth more than two times! That's because your circulatory system is about **66,000 miles** long.

"WAIT—IS THAT MY VOICE?!"

If you've never heard the sound of your own voice recorded and played back to you, you're in for a treat…if that treat were fried eyeballs wrapped in cat fur. Yep, the sound of your own voice can sound super gross and really annoying to you.

"Do you mean my voice sounds different outside my own head?" you might ask, worried.

Don't worry, most people don't like the sound of their own voice. That's because when we speak, we hear it in two different ways all at once:

FROM YOUR MOUTH TO YOUR EARS, JUST LIKE OTHER PEOPLE HEAR IT

RATTLING THROUGH THE BONES OF YOUR SKULL, WHICH GIVES YOUR VOICE A DEEPER PITCH

So get ready for a little torture (but a fun kind of torture)!

WHAT YOU'LL NEED

- Audio recorder; a simple one on a phone will do

WHAT YOU'LL DO

1. Think of a fun phrase to say. Something like, "Chip, chip, cheerio, old pal!" or "He threw three free throws." Or maybe you just want to say something normal and easy, like, "This is how my voice really sounds."

2. Say your phrase out loud.

> **Write down here how your voice sounds to you:**
>
> _____
>
> _____
>
> _____

3. Now hit the record button and say your phrase out loud again.

4. Play it back and listen closely.

> **Write down here how it sounds different than it did the first time:**
>
> _____
>
> _____
>
> _____

Soooo, what do you think of your *real* voice?

MORNING PERSON OR NIGHT OWL?

Animals like squirrels, turtles, and eagles are diurnal, or active during the day. Owls, wolves, and tigers are nocturnal, or active at night. Some animals, like foxes and jaguars, are crepuscular, meaning they are active at twilight periods, in between day and night.

While humans are naturally diurnal animals, some of us prefer a certain time of day. "Morning people" are full of energy early in the day, bolting out of bed like a jolt of electricity. "Night owls" are slower to wake but thrive when the moon is out in a midnight sky. *Hoot hoot!*

Which one are you? If you're not sure, take this quiz to figure it out:

1. When my alarm rings in the morning, I:

☐ **A:** Jump out of bed, ready to hit the ground running.

☐ **B:** Hit he snooze button as many times as I can.

2. I prefer to eat breakfast:

☐ **A:** First thing in the morning, usually by 8 AM.

☐ **B:** Breakfast? No thanks. I'm not hungry that early.

3. I do my homework:

☐ **A:** Right after I get home from school, or right before I go to school in the morning.

☐ **B:** Between dinner and bedtime. My brain works best after warming up all day.

4. If my teacher popped a quiz on the class, I'd hope it would be:

☐ **A:** Before lunchtime.

☐ **B:** After lunchtime.

5. On the weekends, I:

☐ **A:** Can't wait to get up and do fun stuff in my free time.

☐ **B:** Love to sleep in!

6. Bedtime for me looks like this:

☐ **A:** After dinner, I brush my teeth, get into my jammies, curl up with a book, and go to sleep on time.

☐ **B:** I crawl into bed and my mind keeps racing!

If you answered more **A**s, you're a morning person.

If you answered more **B**s, you're a night owl.

GENE MACHINE

Inside almost every cell of your body are genes—so tiny, but so important! Genes work together to make up your genetic code, which is like a set of instructions for building YOU. They are way more complicated than flat-pack furniture instructions, though.

The way you look and, in some cases, the way you are, is determined by your genes. Your genes are passed down to you by your biological parents, which is why you wind up looking like a blend of both of them. You get one set of genes from each of your parents, and this combination determines which traits of theirs you will get. Which genes get passed down is kinda random, actually, and this is how you kinda look like each of your parents.

And to make things a bit more complicated, there are dominant genes and recessive genes. When a dominant gene arm wrestles a recessive gene, chances are the dominant gene is going to win. That's the gene that gets expressed and determines how you look.

Hair color, eye color, height, and whether you can curl your tongue are examples of some of the traits passed down to you though genes. But there are thousands of other things about YOU that were made possible by a wonderful mixture of genes.

Curious about which genes you may have inherited?

A scientific study called The Human Genome Project, conducted between 1990 and 2003, discovered that humans have between 20,000 and 25,000 genes. The combinations of these genes are endless! How's *that* for variety?

WHAT YOU'LL DO

Here is a list of fascinating things that are controlled by genes. See if you've got any of these genes. Then go ask your family if they have them, too.

Tongue-rolling: Can you make your tongue into a tube shape?

Hair on your knuckles

Cleft chin

Eyesight: Do you need glasses? Are you near-sighted or far-sighted?

Extra-long big toe

Achoo Syndrome: Do you sneeze when you look at a bright light?

Bent pinkie finger

Dimples on your face

Hairline shape: Is yours straight across or is yours shaped like a V?

THE CILANTRO TASTE TEST

WARNING: PLEASE MAKE SURE YOU'RE NOT ALLERGIC TO CILANTRO BEFORE YOU PUT IT IN YOUR MOUTH.

Cilantro is a green, leafy herb that grows in gardens and windowsills all over the world. In some places it's called coriander. This herb is featured in dishes of many different cultures, from Mexico to the Middle East to India. People might describe its taste as citrusy, a bit spicy, and… soapy?!

Yep, for some people, putting a cilantro leaf in their mouth is like working up a good lather on the tongue. Gross! Talk about foaming at the mouth…

Why is that? For people who taste cilantro as soap (instead of as *soap*-erior) it all comes down to genetics. Remember those good ole genes? These little bundles of information within the cells of your body determine what you look like, how you experience things, and even how you taste things. There is a small percentage of people who have a variation in a group of genes controlling the sense of smell. These people can taste *aldehydes*, the soapy-flavored chemicals in cilantro. The rest of us don't have that gene variation, so we can't.

Have you ever tasted soap before? No? Oh, good. But have you ever tasted cilantro? Go ahead, give it a try…

So, what does it taste like to you?

ASPARAGUS PEE

To smell pee or not to smell pee—that is the question! At least, where asparagus is concerned.

The vegetable known as asparagus makes your pee smell stinky. When you eat it, your body absorbs and breaks down a certain acid in the veggie that gives your pee a sulfurous odor (that's what the science textbooks call it). Basically, it smells like rotten cabbage.

Anyone who's eaten asparagus for the first time and has NOT been warned of its side effects is in for a weird surprise. Imagine this: You pop a crunchy stalk in your mouth, then have a good chew and swallow. Deeeeelightful! But half an hour later you go to pee and it's stink central!

Or…maybe it's not.

According to research (yes, there are scientists who have researched asparagus pee!), around 50 percent of people cannot smell the stink. Who gets the luck and who doesn't comes down to genetics. I bet you could *not* have guessed that there is a gene for smelling asparagus pee!

So, can you smell asparagus pee, or not?

YOU'VE GOT GOOD TASTE

THIS IS YOUR TONGUE

And this is your tongue on flavor!

There are five known flavors: salty, sweet, sour, bitter, and umami. Your tongue picks up these flavors to help you taste food. It's part of what makes eating a pleasurable experience. In this experiment, you'll find out exactly where your tongue detects each of these five flavors the most.

WHAT YOU'LL NEED

- 5 cotton-tipped sticks
- Salt water
- Sugar water
- Lemon juice
- Slice of onion
- Soy sauce
- 5 colored pencils
- Paper towel

WHAT YOU'LL DO

1. Choose a color to correspond to each of the five tastes. Color in the boxes as your key.

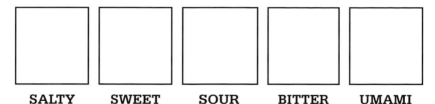

| SALTY | SWEET | SOUR | BITTER | UMAMI |

2. Take your 5 cotton-tipped sticks and dip each one into each of the flavors you have in front of you: salt water for salty, sugar water for sweet, lemon juice for sour, onion for bitter, and soy sauce for umami.

3. Concentrating on one taste at a time, take a cotton-tipped flavor stick and lightly touch your tongue with it in all different locations: tip, sides, middle, and all the way at the back (be careful not to make yourself gag).

4. In between each taste, drink some water to get rid of the last flavor and start again fresh with a new flavor.

5. As you move the cotton-tipped stick around your tongue, notice where the taste is strongest. Fill in that part of your tongue map with that taste's corresponding color.

6. Do this with all five flavors until you have completed your tongue map.

7. Now try doing all this with a dry tongue. Wipe the saliva off your tongue with a paper towel and repeat the taste test above. Can you taste anything? Is it hard? Saliva helps dissolve the chemicals in food that bring out their taste. No saliva = no flavor!

What's **umami**? No, it's not a cool new nickname for your grandmother. It's one of the **five** basic tastes, alongside **salty**, **sweet**, **bitter**, and **sour**. It's described as "meaty" and "savory," and usually leaves you wanting more! Foods like tomatoes, mushrooms, aged cheese, and steak carry the taste of **umami**. Soy sauce has it, too, which is why it was used in this experiment.

TASTE WITH YOUR NOSE!

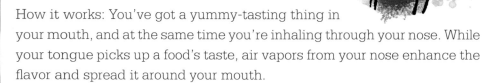

Scientists say that to get the full experience of taste, you've gotta get your nose involved. Your tongue picks up taste, sure, but your nose brings on the flava.

How it works: You've got a yummy-tasting thing in your mouth, and at the same time you're inhaling through your nose. While your tongue picks up a food's taste, air vapors from your nose enhance the flavor and spread it around your mouth.

Think you can taste without getting your nose involved? Test it out!

WHAT YOU'LL NEED

- Some yummy-flavored jelly beans

WHAT YOU'LL DO

1. Have someone else choose a jelly bean for you. Make sure they note the flavor of it but don't tell you what it is.

2. Hold your nose tightly and place the jelly bean in your mouth.

3. Notice the taste of it and write it down.

4. Keeping the jelly bean in your mouth, let go of your nose.

5. Inhale through your nostrils with the jelly bean in your mouth (be careful not to do this too hard or you'll choke!).

6. Notice the taste of it and write it down.

What did you notice about the flavor in your mouth when you let go of your nose and breathed in?

WHAT DOES TASTE FEEL LIKE?

When you eat, the texture of food is also important. Texture is the way a thing feels. Tortilla chips are crunchy. A candy bar is chewy. Peanut butter is sticky. Mashed potatoes are lumpy (or mushy). A smoothie is, well, smooth. You see where this is going…

Do you know which textures you like and which ones you hate?

WHAT YOU'LL NEED

- Blindfold
- 5-6 foods with different textures (such as mushy oatmeal, crunchy carrots, chewy granola bar, hard lollipop, smooth yogurt, lumpy mashed banana)

PLEASE FEEL FREE TO SUBSTITUTE ANY OF THESE FOODS FOR SOMETHING ELSE OF THE SAME TEXTURE, ESPECIALLY IF YOU'RE ALLERGIC!

WHAT YOU'LL DO

1. Put on the blindfold.

2. Have someone else feed you each food one at a time, in a random order. Move the food all around your mouth and chew slowly. Pay attention to how it feels. Finish chewing and swallowing before you put the next food in your mouth.

3. If you don't like the texture of something, spit it out and write down what it was in the space below.

4. If you really like the texture of something, eat more of it!

My least favorite food and texture was:

My favorite food and texture was:

DYE YOUR POOP PINK

How long does it take you to digest a piece of food? Scientists say that it takes between six to eight hours for something you eat to pass through your stomach and your small intestine. It then takes about thirty-six hours to move through your large intestine. All in all, it takes between two and five days for your food to complete the entire process of digestion (depending on the person) and…well…exit as poop.

But wouldn't it be more fun to test this out yourself?

If you were able to stretch out and measure your small and large intestines, they would be about

TWENTY-FIVE FEET LONG

in total. That's almost as long as a school bus!

WHAT YOU'LL NEED

- Beets. Lots and lots of beets.

WHAT YOU'LL DO

1. All you gotta do is eat some beets. Really.
2. Make a note of what date and time you ate those beets.
3. Keep your eyes open for a magical surprise!

Okay, so that's all a bit mysterious, but here it is all laid out for ya: Beets can color your pee and poop pink! If you eat a lot of them, their pigment (or coloring) might not get absorbed by your stomach and intestines, like most nutrients do. That means the red beet color will come out with your bodily waste. It's not entirely clear how or why this happens in the body, and only about 10–14 percent of people experience this colorful toilet surprise. If beets don't turn your poop pink, you could try cherry Jell-O or even tomato soup!

So, did your beet experiment turn your pee or poop pink? How long did it take from the time you ate the beets? That's about how long it takes for food to travel from your mouth to your "other end."

MY SPECIAL FACE

So, you probably know by now that you are one unique creature. A special unicorn. A mystical centaur. A soaring phoenix.

Your genetic code is unlike anyone else's in the world (unless you're an identical twin). You can move your body in very interesting ways. Your senses of taste and smell, and also your voice, are all your own. But the thing that is possibly the most distinct about you is...

YOUR FACE!

WHAT YOU'LL NEED

- This book
- Mirror
- Pencil
- Yourself

WHAT YOU'LL DO

Put your face in front of a mirror and look closely. What do you notice about it? Ask yourself these questions and write down the answers below.

Are your eyes the same size? What color are they?

_____

Is your smile straight or crooked? What about your frown?

_____

Do you have long or short eyelashes? Are they the same color as your hair? What color are your eyebrows?

_____

Are your ears at the same level, or is maybe one higher than the other? Are they attached to your head at the bottom or do your earlobes hang free? (That's another genetic trait!)

_____

_____

What texture and color is your hair? What style are you wearing it in today?

_____

_____

What color is your skin?

_____

Do you have freckles or moles?

_____

What shape is your face: round, oval, heart-shaped, square, rectangular, diamond, triangle? None of these?

_____

_____

What do YOU think is most special about your face?

_____

_____

What do you love about your face?

_____

_____

NOW TAKE OUT YOUR DRAWING MATERIALS ...

Draw a self-portrait of your face while looking only at your face (don't look at the page!) and keeping your pencil on the paper the whole time.

Draw another self-portrait of your face, very slowly and carefully, while constantly looking back and forth between the mirror and your paper.

FUNKY FACE

Stay in front of that mirror, and let's see how many wacky things you can do with your face!

WHAT YOU'LL NEED

- Mirror
- Yourself

WHAT YOU'LL DO

Looking in the mirror, notice if you can:

1. Wink your left eye.
2. Wink your right eye.
3. Raise only your left eyebrow.
4. Raise only your right eyebrow.
5. Wiggle your ears.
6. Touch your tongue to the tip of your nose.
7. Roll your tongue.

   (Remember the gene that allows or doesn't allow you to do this?)

If you can't do some of these funky face moves yet, try to train yourself to do some of them. Skedaddle over to Part 3: Noggin and learn how!

BODACIOUS BOD

Move back from the mirror so you can see your whole body.

WHAT YOU'LL NEED

- Full-length mirror
- Yourself

WHAT YOU'LL DO

Put yourself in front of your mirror and look at your body. What do you notice about it? Ask yourself these questions and write down the answers below:

Are your arms the same length? How many do you have?

Are your legs the same length? How many do you have?

_____

_____

_____

Are your fingers short or long? How many fingers do you have? How about your toes?

_____

_____

_____

What do you notice about your feet? Do they point directly forward, or maybe they are naturally turned in or out?

_____

_____

Do you think you are short, tall, or average height for your age?

_____

_____

_____

What shape is your body: round, square, pear, hourglass, lanky?

_____

_____

_____

Do you have any unique birthmarks or scars?

_____

_____

_____

What do YOU think is most special about your body?

_____

_____

_____

What do you love about your body?

_____

_____

_____

NOW TAKE OUT YOUR DRAWING MATERIALS ...

Draw a self-portrait of your whole body while looking only in the mirror (don't look at the page!) and keeping your pencil on the paper the whole time.

Draw another self-portrait of your whole body, very slowly and carefully, while constantly looking back and forth between the mirror and your paper.

SLOW YOUR ROLL

Okay, time to switch yourself from daytime mode to sleep mode. Having trouble doing this, Kid-Bot 3000™? Try out all of these bedtime relaxation techniques and see which one works best to help you power down at the end of the day.

GET THE WIGGLES OUT

What should you do if it's nearly bedtime and your body feels like it's on a trampoline? We've all been there before. Just wiggle it out!

WHAT YOU'LL DO

1. Get into your comfiest pajamas.

2. Close your bedroom door. You might want some privacy for this Wigglefest.

3. See if you can hold completely still for five seconds, then...

4. Wiggle your butt off! Dance, shimmy, shake, bounce—do whatever moves feel best to you.

5. Then stop! Hold still for another five seconds, then...

6. Start your Wiggle-palooza again!

7. Repeat this as many times as it takes for you to get all those wiggles out of your body.

8. Then flop on your bed and start a-snorin'.

SCRUNCH & RELEASE

Tightening up all your muscles, then releasing them one by one, can be a very relaxing bedtime exercise. Imagine yourself as a hard piece of pasta that gradually softens in hot water. This is also a great way to notice and thank each separate part of your body.

WHAT YOU'LL DO

1. Lie down in your bed and fidget until you're comfortable.

2. Scrunch up and tighten every muscle of your body, even your face. Even your butt!

3. Now relax only your toes and feet and say, "Thank you, feet."

4. Next, relax your leg muscles and say, "Thank you, legs."

5. Continue relaxing each muscle group one by one, moving up your body in this order: your butt, tummy, shoulders, arms, hands and fingers, then face. As you release each muscle, remember to say "thanks" (especially to your butt).

6. If there are any parts of your body that still feel a bit tight, repeat the exercise for these spots.

7. Once your body is completely relaxed, take a moment to breathe long, slow breaths. You should drift off to Snoozeville in no time.

EASY BREATHE-Y

Sometimes all it takes is some calming breaths to relax your body. Try this breathing exercise to see if it properly preps you for bedtime.

WHAT YOU'LL DO

1. Lie down in your bed and clear your mind of the day's thoughts.

2. Breathe out all the air that is in your body, pretending you're deflating a balloon all the way.

3. Then breathe **in** as you count veeery slooooowly 1...2...3...4...5... Fill yourself up with air.

4. Now breathe **out** as you count veeeeery slooooowly 1...2...3...4...5... Empty out all the air from your body.

5. As you do this, make sure you take long, slow, even breaths. This should calm your body and slow your heart rate enough to send you off on the Dream Train, baby.

VACATION IN YOUR MIND

Need a more relaxing place than your bedroom? Take a vacay any day...in your own head!

WHAT YOU'LL DO

1. Lie down in your bed, close your eyes, and think about the most peaceful place you've ever visited. Is it a tropical beach? A mountaintop? A misty lake at dawn?

2. Now bring yourself there by placing a picture of it in your mind.

3. What does the air feel like? What does this place smell like? Are you eating anything? Are you doing an activity? What are you enjoying the most? Really paint this scene for yourself. The deeper you go into this vacation in your mind, the harder it is to leave and the more relaxing it will be for you.

4. Stay on this vacation in your mind until you drift off to sleep on a happy cloud.

Which bedtime body experiment worked best for you?

SLEEP DIARY

Why not keep an eye on your sleeping habits? After all, getting enough good rest is super important for a healthy body. It might be interesting to know more about your bedtime-self, in order to make sure you're getting your best rest.

WHAT YOU'LL NEED

- Diary-style book, with pages showing the days of the week
- Pen or pencil
- Clock

WHAT YOU'LL DO

1. In your new sleep diary, every night make a note of:

- What you do for the hour before bed
- The time you get into your bed

2. Every morning, make a note of:

- The time you wake up
- Whether you fell asleep right away the night before
- Whether you have an easy or hard time getting out of bed
- Whether you had any dreams you can remember

3. Do this every day for a week, and then look back on your sleep diary to ask yourself:

- Which nights did you get the most sleep?
- Which nights did you have trouble falling asleep and/or waking up?
- Do you notice whether your activity before bed affects your sleep?

4. After the first week is complete, try changing your bedtime habits and see if you get better sleep the next week.

5. Continue tracking your sleep as long as you like!

Dear Sleep Diary,

Tonight I switched off my video game at 8:15 PM and started getting ready for bed. I put on my dinosaur pajamas, brushed my teeth with my electric toothbrush, and said good night to my family. Now I'm sitting in my bed writing to you, and I'm feeling wide awake. I hope I can get to sleep okay. I'll tell ya in the morning!

Love,
Me

PART 2

ALL THE FEELS

Now it's time to dive deep...into your innermost feelings: joy, anger, excitement, sadness, anxiety, jealousy, pride, embarrassment—you name it, you've probably felt it.

In this part you'll discover and name your feelings, which can help you understand yourself better. Get ready to take the plunge into the deep sea of emotions and find out more about YOU in the process.

As you swim through this emotional sea, remember that it's all right to feel every wave that washes over you. All feelings are totally normal, and it's okay to feel every single one of them.

Mental health is super important, and so is being able to surf the highs and lows of life. And once you can better understand your emotions and why you're feeling them, you can be there to support yourself and others. Kind of like a feelings lifeguard!

Everyone experiences emotions differently. Some of these experiments might feel difficult for you, depending on your current mood and/or past experience. If any make you feel uncomfortable, skip 'em.

Flip the page to flip out, calm down, make a mistake, be an emoji, and breathe (*whoooossshhh*) through all the feels!

EMOTIONAL VOCAB

Sometimes the hardest thing to do is explain how you're feeling. When you're upset or angry, you might get flustered and fumble for the right words. Or worse: You might shout something you don't really mean and will definitely regret later.

You're not alone! It's really difficult to find the right words in a moment of intense feelings. So why not practice writing down what certain feelings mean to you? Create your very own Feelings Dictionary here.

WHAT YOU'LL DO

1. Get out your favorite pen. You know, the one with a colorful gel tip that sparkles. Or that perfect, flowing felt-tip one. Or the pen with the unicorn cap. The one that makes you feel brilliant and your handwriting look magnificent.

2. Define the emotions below in your own words:

HAPPY:
_____

SAD:
_____

ANGRY:
_____

FRUSTRATED:
_____

ANNOYED:

_____

HURT:

_____

SCARED:

_____

BRAVE:

_____

WORRIED:

_____

BORED:

_____

CONFUSED:

_____

PROUD:

_____

SURPRISED:

_____

HOPEFUL:

_____

LOVING:

_____

EXCITED:

_____

LONELY:

_____

JEALOUS:

_____

EMBARRASSED:

_____

BORED:

_____

SHY:

_____

CURIOUS:

_____

3. Think about times when you've felt some of these emotions. What caused the emotion? What was your experience of the emotion?

COLOR YOUR FEELINGS

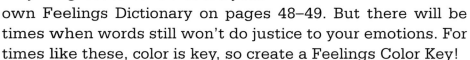

Throughout this section, you'll be exploring your feelings. This is why it's great to have created your own Feelings Dictionary on pages 48–49. But there will be times when words still won't do justice to your emotions. For times like these, color is key, so create a Feelings Color Key!

WHAT YOU'LL NEED

- Crayons, colored pencils, or markers

WHAT YOU'LL DO

1. In this experiment, you're going to assign a color to each of the emotions opposite. Don't be afraid to experiment here, mixing colors together if you think a certain feeling calls for it.

2. What color represents each of these emotions to you? Color in the boxes on page 51.

HAPPY	**SAD**	**ANGRY**	**FRUSTRATED**
ANNOYED	**HURT**	**SCARED**	**BRAVE**
WORRIED	**BORED**	**CONFUSED**	**PROUD**
SURPRISED	**HOPEFUL**	**LOVING**	**EXCITED**
LONELY	**JEALOUS**	**BORED**	**SHY**
CURIOUS	**EMBARRASSED**		

Are you surprised by any of your color choices?

Refer back to this page to help you with any of the experiments in this book.

BREATHE THROUGH IT, BABY!

Just like you tried to slow your roll before bedtime on pages 40–43, breath exercises can calm and support you when you're feeling worried, angry, frustrated, or scared. Try out all of these breathing techniques and see which one works best for you.

LION BREATH

This one might make you feel a little silly, since it requires doing a funny face. Laughter and some roaring are sure to help you get rid of tension!

WHAT YOU'LL DO

1. Sit in a comfortable position: On your knees or cross-legged on the floor are good options.

2. Straighten your arms and rest your hands on your knees in front of you. Close your eyes gently.

3. Take a deep breath through your nose.

4. Open your mouth wide, stick out your tongue, and exhale fast and strong, making one "HA!" sound as you do.

5. While you exhale, bug out your eyes and look toward the tip of your nose.

6. Return your face to a resting position and inhale again.

7. Repeat this breath as many times as you like. You're king of the jungle, after all!

OCEAN BREATH

You can get tossed around by your emotions, or you can ride the waves. Try out Ocean Breath to hear the calming hush of the sea.

WHAT YOU'LL DO

1. Sit in a comfortable position as you did for Lion Breath.

2. Straighten your arms and rest your hands on your knees. Close your eyes gently and keep your mouth open.

3. Take a few long, full breaths, in and out through your mouth.

4. Pay attention to the way your breath feels and sounds as it travels through your throat.

5. On your next exhale, tighten your throat a little and breathe out as if you're fogging up a window. It should make a light hissing noise.

6. On your next inhale, keep this same tightening of your throat as you breathe in. You should hear that light hissing sound again.

7. Once you've done this hissing breath with your mouth open a few times, try doing it with your mouth closed.

This is called **Ocean Breath** because it sounds like some of the noises the ocean makes.

3-4-5 BREATH

Who knew counting could be so relaxing? This breathing technique is surprisingly simple, and oh so soothing.

WHAT YOU'LL DO

1. You can do this breathing technique anywhere. Sure, it'll feel best when sitting or lying down. But you could also do it in your classroom, the mall, before a big exam, or whenever you need to calm down.

2. Breathe out the air that is in your body, deflating your lungs all the way like a balloon.

3. Then breathe **in** as you count to three. Fill up your lungs with air.

4. Next, hold that breath at the top while counting to four.

5. Now breathe **out** as you count to five, emptying all the air from your body.

6. Repeat this several times. How do you feel?

SQUARE BREATH

Like square dancing, this breathing is fun and rhythmic. Unlike square dancing, you don't need a partner for this do-si-do.

WHAT YOU'LL DO

1. Place your finger on the bottom-left corner of the square below.

2. Trace your finger up the left edge of the square as you breathe in slowly while counting to four.

3. Trace your finger along the top edge of the square as you hold your breath while counting to four.

4. Trace your finger down the right edge of the square as you breathe out slowly while counting to four.

5. Trace your finger along the bottom edge of the square, counting to four while you rest.

6. Continue tracing the square and breathing in this way. If you're away from this book and want to do this breathing exercise, trace an invisible square on your palm, or any surface in front of you.

WHICH OF THESE BREATHING EXERCISES DID YOU LIKE BEST?

MOUNT MEDITATION

Now you can describe your feelings *and* breathe calmly and clearly. Put on your active gear and lace up your hiking boots—get ready to climb Mount Meditation! (Actually, just put on comfy clothes and slippers for this one.)

WHAT YOU'LL DO

1. Sit in a comfortable position on a chair, your bed, or the floor. A quiet and peaceful place is best for meditation.

2. Do your favorite breathing technique from pages 52–55 until your body is relaxed. Then change to a slow, quiet breath.

3. Focus on the sound of your breath to clear your mind. If a thought creeps in, acknowledge it, then send it away.

4. Pay attention to how you're feeling in this moment.

5. Once you discover your feeling, say in your head, "I feel _____." Say this a few times.

6. Then take it one step further and say, "I feel _____ because _____." Say this a few times.

7. If your feeling is a bit negative, go one step further and say, "I feel _____ because _____, but I will not always feel this way." Say this as many times as you need to before moving on.

8. Then finish by saying, "I feel _____ right now, and that is okay."

Meditation is a mental and spiritual exercise in which you sit very still and relax, banishing all conscious thoughts from your mind.

EMOTIONAL BLOCKS

A "block" can be something that stands in your way. But these blocks will help you rebuild when you're feeling down.

WHAT YOU'LL NEED

- Wooden blocks (or pieces of paper will do)
- Large sack that is not see-through
- Pen
- Colored pencils
- Piece of paper

WHAT YOU'LL DO

1. Take your wooden blocks and write different emotions on them.

2. Place these blocks into your sack and shake them around.

3. Pull a block out of the bag, look at the emotion you picked, and write down what it is.

4. Think about a time when you've felt that emotion and write something about that experience next to the word.

5. When you've done this with every block, pick a color to represent the feelings you DON'T like. Underline those feelings with that color.

6. Pick a different color to represent the feelings you DO like. Underline those feelings with that color.

7. Next to the emotions you DON'T like, write down some things that stopped you feeling that emotion in the past.

8. Next to the emotions you DO like, write down some things that have helped create that feeling in the past.

9. Keep this list handy, and look at it when you need to.

HUMAN EMOJI

What's your favorite emoji? Is it 😂? Maybe you're more of a 😍 throwing a little 🖤 to your friends and fam. Perhaps today you feel more 🫤. Or are you on 🔥? Mosey on up to a mirror and get ready to become…A HUMAN EMOJI!

WHAT YOU'LL NEED

- Mirror
- Drawing implement

WHAT YOU'LL DO:

1. Look in a mirror and relax your face entirely. What do you look like with a blank face?

2. Now you're going to make some faces in the mirror based on different emotions, then draw each one as an emoji in the boxes provided.

Close your eyes and think about something super gross, like a bowlful of boogers or a dog eating some poop. (What?! They really do it!). Make sure you're really grossed out, then open your eyes and look in the mirror. What face are you making?

Close your eyes again and think about something sad, like your turtle running away or never getting to eat pizza ever again (sob!). Then open your eyes and look in the mirror. What face are you making? Did you make yourself cry?

This time, close your eyes and think about your most embarrassing moment, one that makes you cringe so hard. Then look back in the mirror. What does your so-embarrassed-I-want-to-crawl-into-a-cave face look like?

Close your eyes again and think about something funny, like the best joke you ever heard (probably not a "knock, knock" joke). Have you made yourself laugh yet? Good! Open your eyes to look in the mirror and see what your face is like now.

3. What was your favorite facial expression that you made? Draw a star next to it!

FEELINGS BINGO

As you go through your week, draw an X on every emotion you feel. See if, by Friday, you get five words in a row, either going down, across, or diagonally—BINGO!

HAPPY	SAD	ANGRY	FRUSTRATED	ANNOYED
SCARED	BRAVE	WORRIED	RELAXED	BORED
CONFUSED	PROUD	★	SURPRISED	HOPEFUL
EXCITED	LONELY	GUILTY	EMBARRASSED	JEALOUS
TRUSTING	CURIOUS	CRANKY	IMPATIENT	CHEERFUL

FOREST BATHING

There is an awesome tradition in Japan called "forest bathing," or *Shinrin-yoku* in Japanese. During forest bathing, a person walks through nature in a very mindful way and tries to take in all the peace and wonder around them. It's called "bathing" because you soak up the beauty of nature. This is a meditation practice, kind of like the one you did on page 56. But this time you'll be outside and definitely *not* sitting still. If you have a forest nearby, that's great. But if not, go to your closest green space to do some forest bathing.

WHAT YOU'LL DO

1. Leave your screens at home! No interruptions, please.

2. Go to your nearest, greenest space and find an easy trail to follow.

3. Take a deep breath in through your nose. What do you smell? How does the air feel?

4. Now walk slowly and take careful steps. Feel the trail under your feet. Is it muddy and soft? Is it dry and hard? Do your feet crunch on fallen leaves?

5. As you walk, keep taking deep breaths. This will slow the pace of your walking and relax your body so you can "soak" up nature.

6. Then stop in the middle of your forest. Keep still and stay as quiet as you can. Close your eyes for a moment to see how that changes your experience.

7. Open your eyes again and use your sight, hearing, touch, and smell to sense everything about the forest and let it seep right in. *Ahhhh...*

THE POWER OF Y<u>ET</u>!

Maybe you want to be an astronaut, but you're afraid of heights. Or climb Mount Everest, but you're not strong enough. Or deep-sea dive with sharks, but you can't swim. The *I Can't*s can be much more powerful than the *I Cans*...but only if you let them!

Some things take time to learn and master. But if you want to do something badly enough, you best believe you will. So, when you get frustrated by something you can't do, tell yourself, "I just can't do it ...YET!"

WHAT YOU'LL DO

1. Right here, list some things you want to do, but can't do YET.

_____

_____

_____

2. Now write down what you need to make sure that you can eventually do each of the things listed above. Some of these might be things like "grow up," "learn a new skill," or "be open to new things."

_____

_____

_____

3. Answer these questions to see if you've got the Power of YET!

How do you feel when something is difficult?

_____

_____

What do you do when faced with a challenge?

_____

_____

Was there ever a time when you thought something was difficult, but later mastered it?

_____

_____

Having a growth mindset means you stretch yourself to do new things, even when it's hard.

YOU'RE THE TOPS

Now that you know you CAN do absolutely anything, why not list the things you're already totally tops-tacular at doing?

Celebrate your special powers! Honor your handwriting! Praise your pumpkin-carving! Cheer your cartwheeling! Call yourself the captain!

What do you think you're the best at?

My best subject in school is:

_____

My body is best at doing:

_____

My best feature is:

_____

The best thing about my personality is:

_____

My most unique talent is:

_____

My best shower sing-out-loud song is:

_____

The most creative thing I ever did was:

_____

_____

_____

_____

_____

_____

_____

I can always spell _____ correctly.

Whenever I draw _____ it looks professional.

PS: It's okay to think you are already totally awesome. It's also okay not to be "best" at everything, or even at anything.

I am best at celebrating:

_____

_____

Now, can you think of some things you are second-best at? List them here:

_____

_____

_____

_____

Choose one of these second-best things and see if you can work to make it a top-best thing!

I'M GOING TO WORK TO MAKE

THIS

MY TOP-BEST THING!

_____

_____

_____

DANCE LIKE NO ONE'S WATCHING...

...literally, darling, because *no one will be watching*.

Go to your bedroom, or any space where you can have privacy. Close the door and curtains, and crank up your favorite tunes. Wear headphones if you want this to be a totally undercover sesh.

Now DANCE!

Do the funkiest moves you can think of. Put your hands in the air. Shake from side to side. Roll, thump, swing, bump! Let your body sweat and your spirit shine. Leave your worries behind. Pure movement gets you out of your head and into the present moment.

Which dance move makes you feel like the truest version of you?

BONUS!

Make a playlist of "Feel Good" songs that you can blast whenever you need a dance break.

PERFECTLY IMPERFECT

Speaking of trying to be the best, let's talk about perfection.

Perfection is a tricky thing. Almost everybody wants to be perfect, and lots of people try to get there. But, guess what? Perfection is not even a thing humans can be! It's actually impossible. Even the most perfectly-perfect person is not really perfect at all. (Here's where you insert the joke, "Except for me!" and we all roll our eyes.)

If you did manage to become "perfect," you wouldn't need to strive for anything else in life. Umm, what fun would that be? Perfectly no fun at all.

And check it out: Great things can come from mistakes! Here are a few amazing things you know of that exist because of a mistake:

Can you imagine a world without potato chips? Didn't think so. Now go ahead and make some awesome mistakes of your own.

WHAT YOU'LL NEED

- Pencil
- Markers
- Paints

WHAT YOU'LL DO

1. Close your eyes and draw a line, a squiggle, a shape, or make a splotch of paint below:

2. Open your eyes. What did you make? A fantastic mistake!

3. Now, using your art supplies, find a way to turn that "mistake" into something really cool. If you drew a squiggle, add things to create a scene. If you made a shape, maybe you can turn that into a vehicle. If you splotched paint on the page, try turning it into a cool new creature entirely made up by your perfectly imperfect imagination.

What are some other times when you've turned a mistake into a masterpiece?

GIVE YOUR WORRY 10 MINUTES

All your feelings deserve to be fully felt, no matter whether they're positive or negative. Even worries should be worried over...but just for a little while.

Worry, do your worst! But only for ten minutes.

WHAT YOU'LL NEED

- Timer
- Your worry
- Pen
- Blank paper

WHAT YOU'LL DO

1. At the top of your piece of paper, write down the thing you'll be worrying about right now.

2. Set your timer for ten minutes, and ten minutes only!

3. During these ten minutes, allow yourself to really dwell in your worry: Think about it, write about it, draw it out, and cry or scream about it.

4. When the timer rings, do your favorite calming breath exercise from pages 52–55. Then throw out your worry, walk away, and go about your lovely day.

Did it feel good to give your worry its time and place, and then say, "See ya lata!"?

WORRY STONES

A worry stone is a great thing to keep in your pocket. While this kind of stone can't magically make all your troubles disappear, it does hold a certain kind of power. When you're feeling worried or upset, hold it, rub it, turn it over in your fingers, or step on it with bare feet—all these things can make you feel calm.

Make your own worry stone! Think of something you're worried about right now to write on your worry stone. Naming your worries will help you understand and cope with them. And, if you write them on stones, you can actually leave your worries behind if you want!

WHAT YOU'LL NEED

- Smooth rock or stone that is small enough to fit in your pocket
- Permanent marker
- Acrylic paint
- Paintbrush

WHAT YOU'LL DO

1. Wash your stone and dry it so it's nice and clean.

2. Remember that worry you just identified? Write it on your stone using permanent marker.

3. Now paint your stone with whichever colors you choose. Maybe choose a color that represents your worry.

4. Set the worry stone aside to dry, then keep it close to you so you can reach for it when you need to.

FEAR CRUSHER!

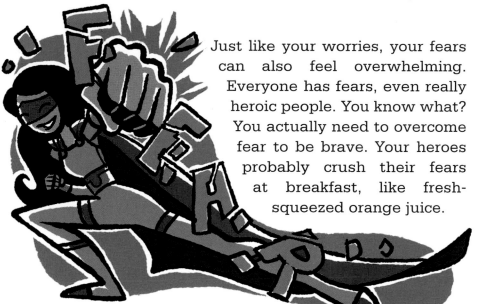

Just like your worries, your fears can also feel overwhelming. Everyone has fears, even really heroic people. You know what? You actually need to overcome fear to be brave. Your heroes probably crush their fears at breakfast, like fresh-squeezed orange juice.

TRASH IT

Go ahead and throw those fears away.

WHAT YOU'LL NEED

- Scraps of paper
- Pencil

WHAT YOU'LL DO

1. Write your fears on little scraps of paper.
2. Throw them in the garbage. Take that, fear!

POP IT

Fears are just full of hot air.

WHAT YOU'LL NEED

- Colorful balloons
- Permanent markers

WHAT YOU'LL DO

1. With an adult's help, blow up your balloons.
2. On each balloon, write the name of a fear you have.
3. Go wild and stomp on the balloons, popping your fear away!

LIGHT IT ON FIRE

Send your fears out to sea and set them aflame, like a Viking.

WHAT YOU'LL NEED

- Rectangular sheet of paper
- Pencil
- Matches

WHAT YOU'LL DO

1. Take your sheet of paper and write one of your biggest fears on it. Now you're going to fold this paper into a boat.

2. Place your paper, fear-side up, vertically in front of you. Fold the paper in half, from top to bottom. Keep it folded for the next step.

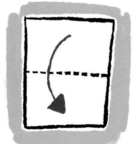

3. Bend the paper in half, this time taking the bottom-right corner over to the bottom-left corner. Make a light crease at the top only, then open this fold back up.

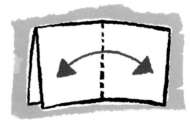

4. Fold the left and right top corners in to the middle crease you made in step 3. You'll now have a sort-of triangle with a double-layered flap sticking out at the bottom. Take the top flap and fold it upward along the bottom edge of the triangle. Make a crease.

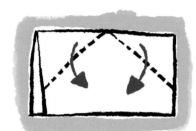

5. Flip the paper over so the other side is now facing up. Fold the other flap upward along the bottom edge of the triangle. Make a crease. You should now have a paper hat.

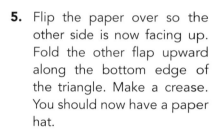

6. Stick your hand into the bottom of the hat and push the sides of the triangle out until it flattens into a square shape.

7. Place your square on the table and turn it 45°, so it's now making a diamond shape with the opening at the bottom. Fold both bottom points of the diamond up to the top points. You should now have a folded triangle with an opening at the bottom.

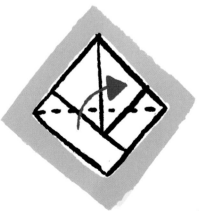

8. Stick your hand into the bottom of the triangle and push the sides out until it flattens into a diamond shape again.

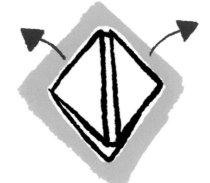

9. Take the two flaps by their top points and pull them out to either side. You should now have a boat with a sail in the middle. This boat will float!

10. Bring your Fear Boat to an open body of water, like a pond, river, or sea.

11. With an adult's help, place the Fear Boat on the water and light it on fire. Then, without getting your face too close, blow the boat out to sea, and wave goodbye to your fear!

Now how do you feel after you've trashed, popped, and burned away your fears?

JAR OF JOY

Since you've gotten rid of some negative feelings, like fear, have you found that there is a bit more room for positive feelings? You'll probably want to keep feelings like joy, excitement, satisfaction, and hope close by. These feelings will need a sparkly, magical place to live, won't they?

WHAT YOU'LL NEED

- Large jar with a lid
- Stickers
- Glue
- Glitter
- Googly eyes
- Pom-poms
- Puffy paint
- Scraps of paper
- Pencil

WHAT YOU'LL DO

1. Decorate your jar with stickers, glitter, paint, and other art supplies. Really go to town making this jar the happiest jar that ever existed.

2. Allow the glue and paint to dry.

3. Whenever something joyful or positive happens to you, write it down on a scrap of paper, fold it up, and place it in the jar. Put the lid on and keep it in a safe place.

4. Go through and read your joyful jottings from time to time, especially when you're having a bad day.

How does it make you feel to write down your moments of joy? How does it feel to read them back to yourself?

FEELINGS BODY MAP

The body is one big conveyor belt for emotional baggage. Check in at the desk and haul your feelings onto the scale, then feel it get carried away to different spots.

Do you get the armpit sweats when you're nervous? Or feel tingles in your legs when you're excited? What happens to your body when you're in a happy mood versus a sad mood?

Label your feelings on this body map, thinking carefully about where you might be sensing each of them. Feelings like anger, anxiety, fear, sadness, excitement, happiness, or embarrassment might make you feel sweaty, shivery, dizzy, or light-headed, or they could give you tummy butterflies, shallow breathing, or a twisted tongue.

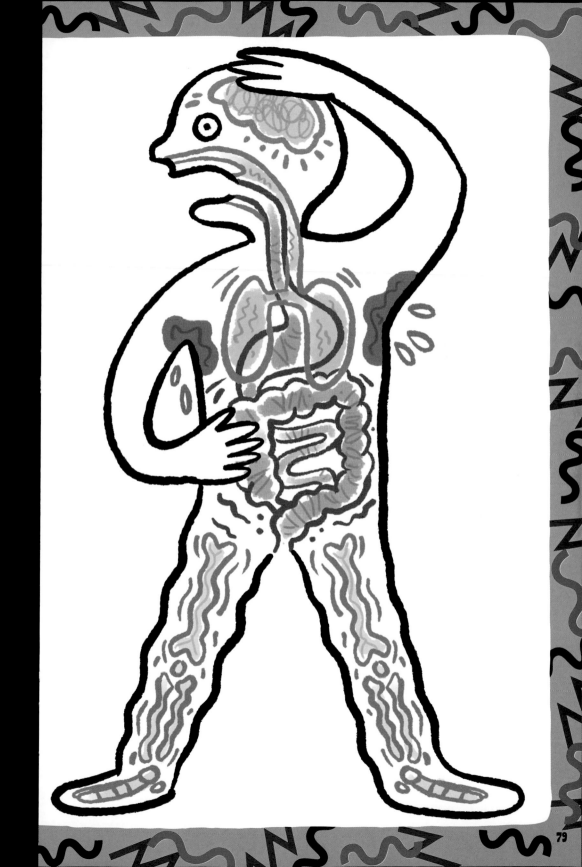

GRATITUDE GRAFFITI

What people, memories, and things are you grateful for? Scribble and draw your gratitude graffiti all over this wall!

Feel free to tear this out and place it somewhere you can always see it.

FACE YOUR FEELINGS

These coping strategies can help you handle feelings of anxiety, anger, or sadness. Try out all of these and see which ones work best for you when facing your feelings.

FOR ANXIETY

- Tap a finger on your forehead
- Rub something soft between your fingers
- Twirl your hair
- Distract yourself with something you like
- Walk backward slowly
- Do any of the breath exercises you've already learned

Draw a star next to the ones that calm your anxiety the most.

MAKE A STRESS BALL

When you're feeling stressed, overwhelmed, or anxious, squeezing something squishy might help! Get a deflated balloon and fill it with sand or rice. Then tie it closed and squeeze out your anxious feelings.

FOR ANGER

- Jump on a trampoline
- Do push-ups
- Grit your teeth
- Scream into a pillow
- Stomp on the ground
- Rip up paper

When you're angry, it's best to do something that does not hurt yourself or anyone else.

FOR SADNESS

- Cry while listening to music
- Dance slowly to a gentle song
- Sing in your room
- Cuddle a pillow or stuffed toy
- Draw something to express your sadness
- Paint your fingernails the color of your sadness

The point is not to conquer your sadness, but to feel yourself move through it to the other side.

ART THERAPY

The world outside can sometimes reflect how we are feeling inside. A stormy sky might resemble anger. A bright yellow leaf might look like happiness. A swirling shell might feel like confusion. Go outside and collect items from the natural world that you can use to paint a landscape of your emotional world.

WHAT YOU'LL NEED

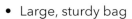 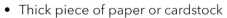

- Large, sturdy bag
- Thick piece of paper or cardstock
- Glue

WHAT YOU'LL DO

1. Grab your large, sturdy bag and head outdoors for a walk.

2. As you walk, think about all the feelings you had this week.

3. Collect items from the ground (do not take live plants or creatures!) that remind you of your feelings. These can be fallen leaves, stones, acorns, shells, fossils, or anything you can see and take with you.

4. Bring them back home and lay them out on a table next to your paper.

5. Arrange the items in a picture of your choice. You might use them to create a self-portrait, a familiar landscape, an abstract collage, a color study of your feelings…whatever makes you feel good!

6. Once you've arranged your creation in the way you like, glue your design to your paper, item-by-item.

What does your nature art say about how you're feeling today?

COMIC STRIP THERAPY

As you probably noticed by doing Art Therapy on the previous page, being creative can help you work through feelings. Now it's time to get a bit more graphic! Use the panels below to create a comic strip of what's happening in your emotional life.

But, let's add a twist! Make your heart, brain, stomach, lungs, eyes, etc. the main characters of your comic strip. What would each of them say to one another when discussing what is happening with your feelings? Draw your characters inside the panels and let their words inside the speech bubbles tell a story of something that recently happened to you.

_____'s COMIC STRIP LIFE

HEART OVER HEAD

When you look at words and images, your brain works quickly to place labels on what your eyes see. Most of the time your brain overrules what your heart feels, like it's the king or something!

What if you took a look with your heart instead of your head? What would it see?

WHAT YOU'LL NEED

- Several magazines and newspapers
- Pencil
- Paper
- Scissors
- Glue

WHAT YOU'LL DO

1. Flip through your magazines and newspapers, cutting out words and images as you go.

2. Put these to the side in one pile and walk away for a bit—long enough to forget about what you cut out. Maybe have a snack or read a book.

3. Then come back to your pile of cutouts.

4. Designate a spot to your left for Pile #1 and a spot to your right for Pile #2. Into Pile #1, you will place all the pictures you associate with happy and easy feelings. Into Pile #2, you will place all the pictures you associate with more difficult feelings, the ones you might need to work through.

5. Take a look at the cutout at the top of your pile, and without giving it much thought, place that cutout into either Pile #1 or Pile #2. Do this as quickly as possible, then move on to the next cutout, placing it into either Pile #1 or Pile #2.

6. Take out your piece of paper and write EASY at the top. Then, flip over the paper and write DIFFICULT at the top.

7. Glue the images and words from Pile #1 underneath the EASY label. Glue the images and words from Pile #2 underneath the DIFFICULT label.

8. When you're done gluing, look closely at the words and images you placed in either category. Ask yourself why certain things might feel easy or difficult to you. Does your brain agree with the decisions your heart just made?

Your heart can tell you what your real feelings are, especially when you don't allow your brain to get in the way!

MY "HAPPY PLACE"

A "Happy Place" is someplace where you feel joyful and content. It's a place you think is 100 percent AWESOME. Thinking about it makes you excited. And actually going there is the *best. Thing. Ever!*

Your Happy Place could be a real place you've been to, a spot you really want to visit, an imaginary place you made up in your mind, or even a moment or memory from your past.

What is your Happy Place? Draw a map of it below:

What do you love about your Happy Place? Write a list here:

_____

_____

_____

_____

_____

Now invite someone special to your Happy Place with this design-your-own postcard:

FEELINGS FIRST AID KIT

Quick—call 911—it's an emergency:

YOU HAVE FEELINGS!

Okay, so having feelings is no reason to call an ambulance. Everyone has 'em, and it's a GOOD thing to let them out when you feel overwhelmed by emotion.

Go ahead: Cry it out, stomp with anger, wriggle with nerves, and flash hot with embarrassment. But do it with a Feelings First Aid Kit by your side!

WHAT YOU'LL NEED

- Medium-sized bag you can zip up and fit into your backpack
- Any of the items you list below

WHAT YOU'LL DO

1. Write down some things that cheer you up or bring you comfort in times of distress:

_____

_____

_____

_____

_____

_____

2. Collect these items and place as many as you can into your ziplock bag. These could be things like an uplifting note from a friend, a picture of a superhero, flavored lip gloss, a piece of candy, a picture of your favorite person, a poem you wrote…anything that brings you solace and joy.

3. Keep your Feelings First Aid Kit in your backpack at all times, and use it when you need to.

4. Feel free to swap out any item that's not doing its job…and place something new into your emergency kit.

Were you surprised by any of the items you chose to put in your Feelings First Aid Kit?

RIGHT HERE, RIGHT NOW

When emotions get heated, they can make you feel as if you're all over the place, instead of right here, right now.

Anger could send you into a fit of white-hot rage. Sadness can bring you down into a dark pit of despair. Anxiety can make you feel like you're in a tunnel. Jealousy can erase the rest of the world except for the object of your jealousy. Feelings are powerful, and they can seem like they control you.

But you've got something even more powerful: mindfulness!

Being mindful means bringing yourself back to the present moment—the right here, right now. And no matter what is happening in your life, right now all that matters is that you are sitting here, you are breathing, you are human, and you exist.

Here is an experiment to bring yourself back to the here and now when a feeling is overwhelming you.

WHAT YOU'LL NEED

- Yourself
- Your breath
- Your five senses

WHAT YOU'LL DO

1. Sit in a chair with your back straight and both feet firmly on the ground.

2. Rest your hands on your knees.

3. Open your eyes and ears.

4. Start doing your favorite calming breath technique from pages 52–55.

5. Without getting up from your chair, pay attention to all five of your senses and identify:

Five things you can see:

1 _____

2 _____

3 _____

4 _____

5 _____

Four things you can touch:

1 _____

2 _____

3 _____

4 _____

Two things you can smell:

1 _____

2 _____

Three things you can hear:

1 _____

2 _____

3 _____

One thing you can taste:

1 _____

Does this help bring you back to the present moment?

PART 3

Are you ready to explore that noggin of yours? This part will be all about that blob of gray matter that keeps your lungs breathing, your heart pumping, your eyes blinking, and your mind thinking. The organ that keeps your whole self fabulous, functioning, and freestyling… Your powerful BRAIN!

Your brain is part of your nervous system, a network of nerves and cells that act like electrical wires sending messages throughout your body. The nervous system controls your movement, involuntary body functions like breathing and digesting food, and senses like touch and sight. Obviously, your brain also makes you think all your thoughts, but it has a much bigger job to do. It keeps your whole body working. That's a lot of responsibility for an organ weighing just three pounds!

Just like no two people are the same, no two brains work the same way, either. Everyone has their strengths *and* weaknesses. It's all okay. Everyone is beautifully brilliant in some way, shape, or form. But if any of these experiments feel difficult or uncomfortable for you, don't do them. Skip to the ones that make you feel like the genius that you are.

Are you ready? Turn the page to break some habits, make memories, explore your dreams, fool your eyes, and play some serious games…with your brain!

BUST THOSE HABITS!

Old habits are hard to break. They hang on to you like a favorite shirt—soft, well-worn, and comfortable. Maybe too comfortable...

Do you always doodle the same thing in the margin of your notebook? To get to school, do you walk the same exact route every day? When you're sad, do you always reach for something sweet to pick you up? Is your bedtime routine the same thing every night? All these things can be comforting, but it's good for your brain to change it up and break habits.

When you do something new, your brain makes a new squiggle, or neural pathway. That's some serious brain growth. When you're a kid, your brain is always making new squiggles because you are constantly seeing and learning new things. But how would you like to help it along? Here are some cool things to try out to break some old habits.

WHAT YOU'LL DO

1. When you're going to school or the park, notice if you always walk the same streets each time. Could you walk another way? Instead of taking your well-worn path, try turning left instead of right, or go straight instead of turning, and take a different street instead.

2. Feeling low? Reaching for your chocolate stash? Try snacking on something else to see if it changes your mood. Eat something salty, crunchy, or sour instead. How does eating each of these make you feel? Try one for today's bad mood, then try a different one for a bad mood in the future.

BRUSH TEETH → **WASH FACE** → **READ BOOK** → **SAY GOOD NIGHT** → **TURN OFF LIGHTS** → **SNORE!**

3. Doing the same thing night after night is boring. Try mixing it up tonight. Brush your teeth first or put on your pajamas last. Just be careful you don't bump into a wall if you're trying to get dressed for bed in the dark!

Which of these things was easiest for you to do? Which was the hardest habit to break?

DREAM DIARY

Dreams are difficult to pin down, especially since you can only remember them some of the time. Your brain makes dreams every single night, during the Rapid Eye Movement, or REM, phase of sleep. REM happens for ninety-minute cycles over and over again, and this is when you dream. So, if you wake up in the middle of a REM cycle, you'll remember the dream you're having. But if you wake up after REM stops, you won't remember the dream.

Have you ever woken up remembering a dream and wondered why your brain just made up all that stuff? Some dreams are boring and some are exciting or strange. Some are totally embarrassing and some are frightening. Since they are produced by your *subconscious* and could contain your innermost thoughts and feelings, dreams may uncover a truth about yourself. Some dreams might help you solve a problem you're facing. Dreams might be the key to understanding your brain a little bit better.

What do YOUR dreams say about you?

WHAT YOU'LL NEED

- Journal to keep by your bed
- Pen to keep next to your bedside journal

WHAT YOU'LL DO

1. The moment you wake up, and before you do anything else, turn to your bedside journal and write down anything you can remember of your dream. Even if it's just a feeling, start writing about it, and you might remember more details.

2. Track your dreams for a week in your journal, writing them down every time you wake up. Try setting an alarm clock to wake you up a little bit earlier than usual. Interrupting your dream cycle could help you remember more dreams.

3. Go back through the week's dream journal and read what you've written. Do you recognize any patterns or repeating themes? Underline anything that comes up more than once.

4. In your dream diary, mark down how many mornings you wake up remembering your dream. Note if your dreams are ever related to something you've experienced the day before. Underline anything that surprised you from your dreams.

5. Feel free to continue your dream journal for as long as you want to.

Sometimes a dream can shock you with a truth about yourself that you didn't yet know.

CHILDHOOD MEMORY GAME

Childhood memories are filled with joy, excitement, confusion, fear, embarrassment, and so many other emotions you explored in Part 2, "All the Feels." Your memories are *yours* to keep, and each one is special because it makes you…YOU!

The cool thing is, you're still making childhood memories every day because, well, you're still a child! When you get to be an adult, it will be fun and interesting to look back on your memories and remember the feeling of being a kid.

Why not help out your (probably forgetful) adult self by creating a special, personal homemade game of Memory using your own childhood memories?

WHAT YOU'LL NEED

- 24 cards that are all the same size and color (try cutting index cards in half)
- Colored pens, pencils, markers, and/or crayons
- Ziplock bag to hold your homemade memory game

WHAT YOU'LL DO

1. In this activity, you'll pair up certain things that spark memories for you. Things like colors, tastes, smells, and songs are powerful triggers for memories. For example, the smell of a certain soap could remind you of a sleepover at a friend's house. Or the smell of a BBQ grilling could remind you of that time you won the final baseball game of the season.

2. Below, write down your twelve most recent memories—one per month for the past year. (Note: They don't all have to be happy memories.)

1 _____

2 _____

3 _____

4 _____

5 _____

6 _____

7 _____

8 _____

9 _____

10 _____

11 _____

12 _____

3. Now, for each memory listed above, write down a color, taste, smell, song, place, or feeling that matches that memory.

- _____
- _____
- _____
- _____
- _____
- _____

- _____
- _____
- _____
- _____
- _____
- _____

4. Take your twenty-four cards and split them up into two sets of twelve.

5. On one set of twelve cards, write out or draw a picture of your memories from the first list.

6. On the other set of twelve cards, write out or draw a picture of your memory trigger from the second list.

7. On the blank side of every card, you can draw a logo for your homemade Memory game, or you might choose to leave them blank.

8. Now, play! Flip all the cards facedown on a table, so the logo or blank side is facing up.

9. Flip over one card, then see if you can find its memory match to flip over. If you don't find a match, flip both cards back to their original positions, blank-side up.

10. Keep playing until you've matched every memory card to its trigger card. You can choose to play the game alone or with someone you love and trust with your memories.

11. When you're finished playing, shuffle your deck and place it in the bag to put away for the next time you want to play.

12. You can add to your Memory deck every year or any time a new memory is made. Keep building up your deck with more and more memories!

TIME CAPSULE

If you were able to talk to Future You, what would you say? What would you show yourself about the life you are living right now? What would you want to remember?

Who do you think you will become in the future? If it's part human, part robot (hey there, Kid-Bot 3000™), you may be right about that. Make a guess and create a TiME Capsule for yourself!

A TiME Capsule (emphasis on the *ME*) is a box full of stuff from right now that you can hide for Future You to find. In this box, you can place handwritten notes, small toys and mementos, snack wrappers, and anything that you think will spark a memory for the future you who will find the box.

WHAT YOU'LL NEED

- Shoebox (or any box of a similar size)
- Paper
- Drawing materials
- Anything you want to collect for the box (see suggestions below)

WHAT YOU'LL DO

1. Open your box and make sure it's clean and empty.

2. Go around your house and collect small items to leave in the box for Future You. These things can be:

   - Small toys
   - Photographs
   - Pictures you drew
   - Lists you made
   - Receipts from things you bought
   - A wrapper from your favorite snack

3. Now, on your paper, write a note to Future You about:

   - The things you like to do
   - Your favorite song, movie, TV show, video game, sport, school subject
   - Your best friends
   - What school is like for you
   - What you think you'll be like when you grow up

4. Place everything in your box and shut it. Maybe even tape it closed.

5. Now hide it somewhere you will forget about it.

6. When you find your box years later as Future You and look through it, you'll be able to discover:

- What was Past You like?
- How have you changed since then?
- Do you still like some of the same things?
- Are you still friends with the same people?
- What memories does the box bring up for you?

By creating your TiME Capsule, what have you learned about yourself through the things you decided to leave for Future You? What do you hope Future You thinks of who you are right now?

THERE'S A STORY IN MY BEDROOM

They say everyone's got a story to tell. Stories live within us and also outside of us. The things you choose to keep tell a story, too. There's probably a story right in your bedroom!

Grab your pen and notebook and get comfy. Empty your mind as much as possible. Then…look.

No, *really* look. What do you notice in your bedroom? After looking for a while, pick three things you see and write them at the top of your page. Bonus challenge: Find something that is very new to you.

Now write a story that includes all three things. It can be long or short. Then, if you're feeling up for it, recite your story to yourself in the mirror.

Think about your story and your three items. How did you weave your items into your story? What was your story about? And what do your three chosen items say about you?

- If you chose an item from nature, you are in tune with the outdoors.

- If you chose an item you bought or made yourself, you are confident.

- If you chose an item that a family member or friend gave you, you care about your relationships.

- If you chose an item that is sport-related, you feel like a winner.

- If you chose an item that is soft and cozy, you like to be comfortable.

- If you chose an item that cannot be categorized, you are very unique!

BODY-BRAIN CONNECTION

Your brain is connected to your whole body through your nervous system. And your nervous system is exactly what it sounds like: It's your body's structure that makes you feel really anxious about monsters. Just kidding! It's a system of nerves and cells throughout your body that send signals to make you sense things and to move.

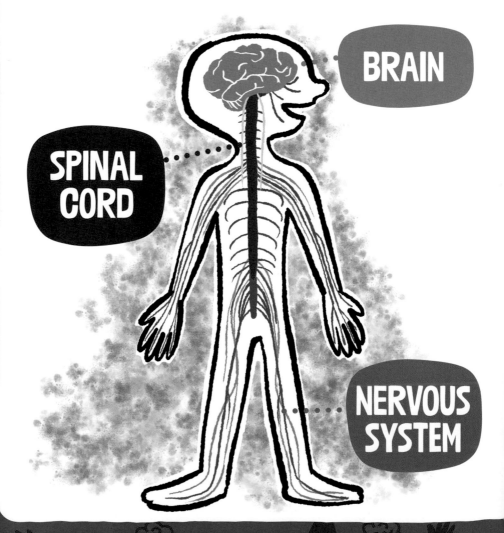

BRAIN

SPINAL CORD

NERVOUS SYSTEM

We're going to pay attention now to the nerves that control your sense of touch. You may have noticed that when you get cut or hit in a certain place on your body, it hurts more than other places. For example, a paper cut on your finger is the worst pain in the world, and hurts *way* more than a graze on your shin. Why is that? Well, certain places on your body have more nerve endings than others. Let's see where YOU are most sensitive:

WHAT YOU'LL NEED

- Something with a point, like a sharpened pencil

WHAT YOU'LL DO

1. Take the tip of your sharpened pencil point, and lightly tap it on your fingertips. Now tap it on the palm of your hand. Now tap it on the back of your hand. Which spot is most sensitive? Mark it here:

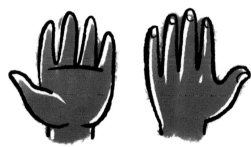

2. Tap the sharpened pencil point on the bottom of your foot, moving it all around. Notice if there are spots on your feet that are more sensitive than others. Now tap the pencil point on the top of your foot. Which spot is most sensitive? Mark it here:

3. Now tap the sharpened pencil point up your leg and up your arm. Where are you most sensitive in these places? Mark it here:

4. Tap the sharpened pencil point all over your belly, avoiding your belly button, please! Mark where you are sensitive on your belly:

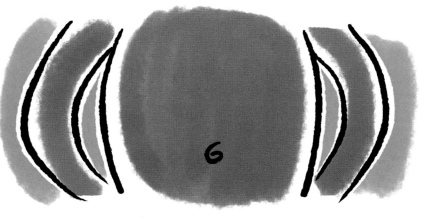

5. Make the final call: Where is your body most sensitive?

CAN YOU FOOL YOUR BRAIN?

You might think your mind is the smartest thing about you: It's your #1 noggin, supreme egg, top thinker, noodle extraordinaire.

You already know each part of your body is attached to your brain through your nervous system. Little nerves in your fingers, feet, and other body parts send messages to your brain to tell you to feel pain, heat, cold, itchiness, and other sensations. Most of the time, this happens so you can stay out of danger and be safe and comfortable. But what if your body could trick your brain?

These cool tactile illusions will show you how easy it is to fool your own brain. Or, do you think you're smarter than all that? Can your brain win over your body? Test it out!

TOUCH A HOT GRILL

This illusion is one hot dog of a trick!

WHAT YOU'LL NEED

- 6 hot dogs
- Freezer
- Microwave

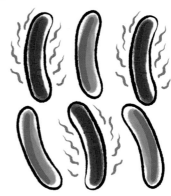

WHAT YOU'LL DO

1. Take three of the hot dogs and place them in the freezer for an hour.

2. About two minutes before you take out the frozen hot dogs, place the other three hot dogs on a microwaveable plate. Put them in the microwave on a low power percentage for one minute, then let them cool for one minute.

3. Take the frozen hot dogs out.

4. Make a pattern on a countertop with your warm and frozen hot dogs: one warm, one frozen, one warm, one frozen, one warm, one frozen.

5. Place your hand on top. How does it feel?

Even though none of the hot dogs was very hot, did your hand feel like it was burning? How? The warm-cold pattern tricks your brain! The extreme cold of the frozen hot dog mimics the pain of touching a searing-hot metal surface. That, coupled with the slightly warm hot dogs, makes you think you're touching a hot grill. Or, smarty-pants—were you able to rationalize that you were only touching frozen and lukewarm hot dogs? Tell the truth!

THREE COLD COINS

This trick is similar to the previous one, but it will further test your brain's ability to tell the difference between cold and heat.

WHAT YOU'LL NEED

- 3 of the same type of coins
- Freezer

WHAT YOU'LL DO

1. Place two of the coins in the freezer for about fifteen minutes. Keep one of the coins on your countertop, at room temperature.

2. When you take the coins out of the freezer, place them on either side of your room-temperature coin. The three coins should form a row.

3. Using your right hand, place your pointer finger on the left coin, your middle finger on the middle coin, and your ring finger on the right coin.

4. How does your middle finger feel?

If your middle finger felt as cold as the other two, you tricked your brain! How did this happen, if that coin wasn't cold? When your three fingers were lined up and touching the coins, the nerve endings were not able to tell the difference between cold and warm. So, your brain filled in the message, but incorrectly!

Or were you able to correct your brain and feel the real temperature of the coin?

CONFUSE YOUR BRAIN TO GET RID OF PAIN

This tactile illusion could be a big help if you step on a sharp toy or get a dreaded paper cut. The next time one of your hands, arms, feet, or legs gets hurt a little bit…do this trick!

Say you've accidentally stubbed your left toe and it really hurts. The toe is throbbing. The feeling is shooting up the nerve and telling your brain you're in pain. Simply sit down and cross your legs so your left toe is now on the right side of your body. This should confuse your brain about which part of your body is in pain, and it will hurt less!

TWO NOSES ARE BETTER THAN ONE

This illusion is said to be one of the oldest tricks in the book! An Ancient Greek philosopher called Aristotle is credited with figuring this out over 2,300 years ago.

WHAT YOU'LL NEED

- Your fingers
- Your nose (eww—not for *that* activity!)

WHAT YOU'LL DO

1. Cross your pointer finger and your middle finger.
2. Stick the tip of your nose in between your two fingers. Does it feel like you're touching two noses?

You can also try this trick with a small round object, like a marble or a pea.

When you do this, your brain forgets that you've crossed your fingers and thinks you're touching two separate objects. That's why you feel like you've got two noses! Or, are you totally convinced that you will only have one nose, forever and ever?

Sometime tactile tricks like this require that you suspend your belief about reality. Are you the kind of person who can do that?

AM I RIGHT...
OR AM I LEFT?

Which side of your body do you favor: your right or your left? You may think the answer is as easy as saying which hand you write with...but think again!

Some theories suggest that if you're "right-brained" you're a more creative person, and if you're "left-brained" you're a more logical person. Just to confuse things a little more, the right side of your brain controls the left side of your body, and the left side of your brain controls the right side of your body. And let's confuse things even more: Many scientists would say that people use both sides of their brain equally, and the right-brained/left-brained theory is a myth.

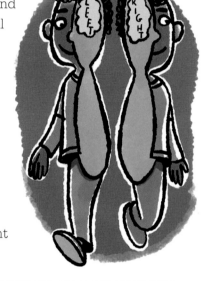

But why don't you try out this experiment to see if you're right...or if you're left.

WHAT YOU'LL DO

1. Interlace your fingers, like this:

2. Which thumb is on top—right or left? Now interlace your fingers again but make sure your *other* thumb is on top. Does it feel weird?

3. Without thinking too much, cross your arms in front of your body. Which arm do you naturally put at the top? Now cross your arms the other way. How does that feel?

4. Give yourself a hug. Go on—love yourself! Which arm do you place on top of the other to wrap around and give yourself a good ole squeeze? Is it the same one that was on top when you crossed your arms?

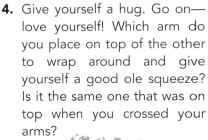

5. Standing up straight, cross your legs and bend down to touch your toes. Which leg do you place in front? Now cross your legs the other way and bend down to touch your toes. Did you wobble or fall over?

6. Pretend you're about to kick a soccer ball, and go for a goal shot. Which foot do you use to kick? Is it the same one you put in front when you first bent down to touch your toes?

Okay, so work it out:
Are you right, are you left, or are you both?

COLOR CONFUSION

Okay, so this is a really fun but really annoying experiment for your brain. Do you know your colors? Well, sure ya do.

But! When you begin, you'll have all the confidence in the world that your brain won't be tricked by what your eyes see. Don't be so sure...

WHAT YOU'LL DO

1. Look at the color word chart below.

2. Go through the rows and columns and name the colors of the words you see. DON'T read the words themselves, but say the color that each word is written in. For example, if you see the word *green* but it's printed in the color blue, say "blue."

3. Name the colors as fast as you can. Ready? Set...GO!

BLUE	**ORANGE**	**BLACK**
RED	**PURPLE**	**WHITE**
BROWN	**YELLOW**	**GREEN**

4. How did ya do? Now try going slower. Did you get more correct this time?

COLOR BLINDNESS

Some people are color-blind, which means they can see things clearly, but not with the full range of colors. A person with full-color vision can see all the colors because their eyes absorb all three light wavelengths: red, blue, and green. But a person who is color-blind may only be able to see one or two of the three light wavelengths. Are you, or someone you know, color-blind? Test it out by trying to find the symbols within the circles below.

SYNESTHESIA SUPERPOWER!

Can you hear the sound of colors? Can you taste a song? Can you smell a word? If so, you probably experience synesthesia.

Synesthesia is when a person's two senses are linked. For example, you might hear a musical note and see a certain color—not just imagine it, but *really* see it. A word might make you able to smell a scent.

Any combination of the senses is possible. Sounds cool, right? Or maybe it smells cool to you! Here's one way to see if you experience synesthesia.

WHAT YOU'LL NEED

- Someone to help you
- Piece of paper
- Pencil

WHAT YOU'LL DO

1. Have your helper choose ten letters of the alphabet in a random order. Your helper will write them down on a piece of paper to keep as the "master list."

2. Now your helper will read the letters out loud to you, at a rate of one every three seconds. For example: *G* (wait three seconds)… *J* (wait three seconds)…*B* (wait three seconds)…

3. After each letter is read out loud, you must write down the letter and the color you associate with it. Don't think about it too much (remember, you only have about three seconds). Just write down the letter and the color.

4. After you've gone through all the letters and you've written down all the colors, put your list aside.

5. A couple of hours later, repeat steps 1–4, but have your helper change the order of the letters.

6. After you've gone through all the letters and you've written down all the colors again, compare your two lists.

7. If you have synesthesia, most or all of your letter-color matches will be the same on both lists.

PART 4

HUMANKIND
HOP
SCO

You've done tons of experiments on your body, feelings, and brain. Now it's time to look outward and discover your humanity. Or wait—are you a Kid-Bot 3000™? Awesome! Whether kid or kid-bot, this part will help you figure out where you fit into this big, beautiful, sometimes scary world. Get ready to learn more about your personality and your place in the world!

Remember that YOU get to choose what, when, and how you present yourself. You decide your personality, how you communicate with people, how far you push yourself in social spaces, and when it's time to retreat to your comfort zone. You also choose how you treat others, and how you let other people make you feel.

Everyone experiences their world differently. Some of these experiments might feel difficult. Feel free to skip any experiments that make you feel uncomfortable and repeat those that make you feel great!

Go on...Turn the page to map out where you belong, fly your flag, test your personality, say "yes," and high-five your way through the world!

TCH

WALLFLOWER OR PARTY ANIMAL?

When you're at a party, do you find yourself in the middle of the action or do you prefer the sidelines? You might be someone who prefers being the center of attention, or you might prefer being alone. Or, you might like both…at different times!

No matter what your personality is like, you are an awesome possum (or other creature of your choice).

Those who are energized by social situations are usually called *extroverts*. And people who are more reserved or quiet in social situations are usually called *introverts*. Which one are you?

Take this quiz to find out! For each scenario, choose which answer fits you best: A, B, or C.

When you have a great idea, you:

☐ **A:** Announce it to the world right away, via megaphone!

☐ **B:** Keep it in your head until you're ready to tell someone you trust.

☐ **C:** Sometimes shout it out loud and sometimes hold it in.

You've been very active all day. By 5 PM, you:

☐ **A:** Feel like running around the neighborhood.

☐ **B:** Feel like taking a nap.

☐ **C:** Feel neither energized nor tired.

In class, your teacher assigns a project for the afternoon. You:

☐ **A:** Jump into it immediately. Learning by doing is your style.

☐ **B:** Pause to think and watch others begin. Learning by observing is your style.

☐ **C:** Start right away, but stop to pause and think at times.

A friend asks you to hang out on Saturday. You:

☐ **A:** Say "yes" right away—how exciting!

☐ **B:** Say you're not sure. You really feel like watching movies alone all weekend.

☐ **C:** Say you'll check your schedule and get back to them.

You feel happiest when you're:

☐ **A:** At a loud, fun party with a lot of people.

☐ **B:** At home, drawing by yourself for hours.

☐ **C:** Out with a couple of really good friends.

Tryouts for the school play are coming up and everyone must participate. You:

☐ **A:** Are going to try out for the lead role. You were born to be onstage.

☐ **B:** Will ask to be part of the costume and set decorating committee. You are happy to work behind the scenes.

☐ **C:** Prefer a small part or to be part of the ensemble. You feel more comfortable in a group.

Your teacher announces the big end-of-year group project. You:

☐ **A:** Can't wait, and hope you get put in a group with all your friends.

☐ **B:** Groan. Group projects are your nemesis.

☐ **C:** Shrug. You guess you have to participate, and hope you get put into a good group.

IF YOU ANSWERED...

Mostly As, you are an extrovert. Extroverts are usually sociable, energetic, loud, and enjoy being with people. They also jump right into things, sometimes without thinking it over first. If you're an extrovert, you probably like being out with large groups of people, trying new things, and interacting with your environment.

Mostly Bs, you are an introvert. Introverts are usually more reserved, less energetic, quiet, and like being alone. They tend to test the waters before getting involved with something...if they get involved at all, that is! If you're an introvert, you probably like hanging out by yourself, doing familiar things, and focusing on the world inside yourself.

Mostly Cs, you are in-between extrovert and introvert, and sometimes flip between the two. Many people fall into this category, avoiding the personality extremes of being an introvert or extrovert.

LOOK THROUGH THE WINDOW

What words would you use to describe yourself? How would others describe who you are? Do you think these two things match up? Test it out!

WHAT YOU'LL DO

1. As you go through the experiment, place all the answers in the grid here:

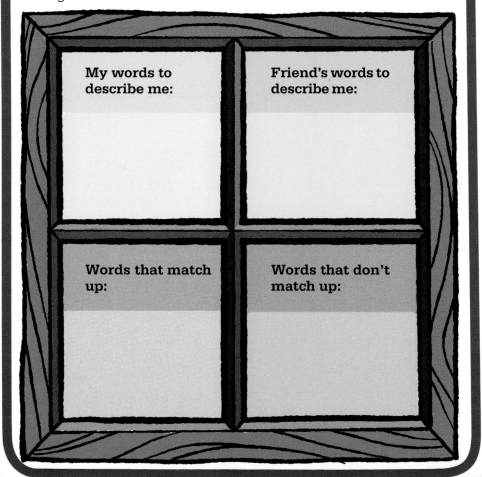

My words to describe me:

Friend's words to describe me:

Words that match up:

Words that don't match up:

2. Choose five or six words from the list below that you think best describe you, and write them in the top-left box in the grid.

FRIENDLY CALM KIND SMART ACCEPTING LOUD

TRUSTWORTHY HAPPY BOLD HELPFUL POWERFUL

FUNNY SHY BRAVE MATURE CONFIDENT

SELF-CONSCIOUS QUIET NERVOUS SILLY

SWEET TENSE ORGANIZED ENERGETIC ATHLETIC

3. Now, without showing your choices, ask your best friend to choose five or six words from the list that they think best describe you. Write them in the top-right box in the grid.

4. In the bottom-left box, write all the words that overlap between what you chose and what your friend chose.

5. In the bottom-right box, write all the words that your friend chose, but you didn't choose.

6. Take a close look at the words in the bottom-left box, the ones that overlap. These are the ways you regard yourself *and* the world regards you. What do you think about these words?

7. Now take a close look at the words in the bottom-right box. These are the ones your friend chose to describe you, but that you would *not* use to describe yourself. Are you surprised? What do you think about these words? Do you agree at all?

8. Try doing this experiment several times, with different friends or family members. What did you learn about how the world sees you? What did you learn about how you see yourself?

**How does it look through your "window"?
Do others see you the same way you see yourself?**

ME LAND

Who ARE you? What is your personality, your likes and dislikes, your accent and language, the way you look and dress? All these things make up who you are, and they are important to know as you start to find your place in the wider world. Take a trip to...ME Land, where you can celebrate what makes you awesomely, uniquely you!

WHAT YOU'LL NEED

- Colored pencils, markers, and crayons
- Stickers
- Safety scissors

WHAT YOU'LL DO

1. On page 132, draw a map of a land that is totally, 100 percent YOU.

2. Include features, like mountains, rivers, valleys, coasts, towns, and cities.

3. Answer these questions:

What are your favorite animals?

_____

What are your favorite shapes?

_____

What are your favorite colors?

_____

What are your favorite words?

_____

What are your favorite foods?

_____

What are your favorite activities?

_____

What are your favorite songs?

_____

What are your favorite shows?

_____

What are your favorite books?

_____

What are your favorite games?

_____

What are your favorite items of clothing?

_____

Do you have an obsession?

_____

Do you have a hobby?

_____

Do you have a collection of something?

_____

What makes you laugh?

_____

What is your happiest memory?

_____

4. Now fill your map with words and drawings of the things you love most.

5. Color it in and decorate it with stickers.

6. Name your land anything you want.

Draw your ME Land here!

FLY YOUR FLAG!

Now that you have established ME Land and claimed it as your own, you're going to need a flag to wave proudly in the breeze.

Your flag for ME Land should be as unique as you are. In order to design your very own flag, think of all your answers from the last experiment, like your favorite animal, color, food, etc.

Choose between 4–6 of those favorite things, and use them to design your flag below.

What is your flag and your land all about? Create a motto, or phrase, for ME Land here:

_____

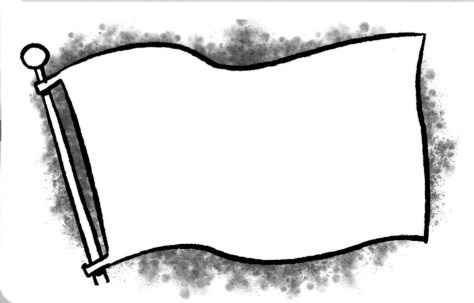

SO STYLIN'

The **way you dress and style yourself shows how you want the world to see you.** It makes up one part of your identity, or personality.

Some kids want to blend in with the rest of the crowd. Others want to be noticed and stand out. Which are you? Or do you flip-flop between the two? Do you wear flip-flops, even in winter?

Let's figure out your "dream look" right here. It can be anything you want it to be. Choose your clothing, hairstyle and color, shoes, and accessories—as funky or formal as you like—and draw it on the figure on the next page. Go for it!

So, is your dream look the real way you present yourself to the world? What are the differences? What are the similarities? Did you draw anything here that surprised you? And what do you have to do to get your "dream look"?

Think about how your look represents your personality.

CULTURE CLUB

It's true that people may be defined by how they present themselves to the world through their clothing and hairstyle. But deeper down, you know that you are so much more than just what you wear. You are also made up of your likes, dislikes, intelligence, sense of humor, how many hot dogs you can eat in one minute (just kidding—please don't try that one at home!), how you treat others, and also—very importantly— who you are culturally. Your cultural identity is a big part of you.

Culture is like your way of life. It is formed by what you believe, where your family comes from, how you speak, what your attitudes and values are, and even what your goals for the future might be. Your culture will likely incorporate your race, ethnicity, and heritage. A lot of your culture comes from your family background.

What's cool is that we learn about our culture throughout life. Do you already know what makes up your culture? Do you want to know more? Try this out to dig deeper into your own culture.

WHAT YOU'LL DO

1. Interview family members about where your family came from. Bring along a pen and notebook, and ask things like:

   - When did you move to where you live now?
   - Who was the first family member to live in this country/city/town?
   - Does our family speak any other languages?
   - What is your favorite word from that language?
   - Can you teach me a family recipe?
   - Can you tell me one of our family jokes or stories?
   - Are there any family sayings or phrases to know about?
   - What is our family's most important tradition?

2. Take what you have learned about your family culture from asking these questions and, on a separate piece of paper, create a map or flag representing everything about where your family is from, like you did with ME Land.

3. Try making your family recipes alongside a family member. Eat them together.

4. If your family speaks a language other than English, learn some of your family's favorite words or phrases in that language.

5. Tell a family joke or story to a friend. Then ask your friend to tell one of theirs, too!

Being of a culture different from your friends and teachers is awesome! You add something special that makes your class extra interesting.

ANIMAL ATTRIBUTES

GRRR… Meow. Woof! ROAR! What is *your* inner animal?

Are you a:

DOG
Very active. Loves to eat. Loyal to best friend.

CAT
Likes to hide. Sometimes sneaky. Purrs when stroked.

SHARK
Out for blood. Amazing swimmer. A bit scary.

CHEETAH
Fast runner. Very fashionable. Enjoys meat.

SLOTH
Sleeps for fifteen hours per day. Vegetarian. Loves Mom.

MONKEY
Likes to hang out. Tree-hugger. Really smart.

LION
Large and in charge. Active at night. Sticks with family.

BUTTERFLY
Loves fresh air. Delicate and beautiful. Able to transform.

Which are you most like? Choose two or three of these animals and draw a creature below that combines their features and characteristics.

This is your mythical sidekick!

THE PATH TO EMPATHY

Empathy is when you can relate to what someone else is feeling. Why is this important? When you empathize with someone, you can remember feeling in the past exactly what they are feeling at that moment. By relating to another person's feelings, you can let them know they are not alone, which can help them feel better. Sometimes empathy makes all the difference!

The path to empathy is paved with feelings! Here's a little experiment to get you inside your own feelings so you can connect with someone else's.

WHAT YOU'LL DO

1. Think of some times when you've felt sad, embarrassed, or angry. For example, "I dropped my lunch tray and everyone in the cafeteria laughed at me," or "A bully found my personal note and shared it with the whole class," or "Someone stole my favorite pen."

2. Write down as many as you can on slips of paper and place them in an envelope. Put this aside for a day or two.

3. When you come back to your slips of paper, read them as if they happened to your best friend. In fact, cross out any "I," "my," and "me" words, and replace them with the words "you" and "your" instead.

4. When you read them back like this, how do you feel? What would you do if you saw these situations happen to your friend? How might you react if you were witnessing instead of experiencing?

HOW DO I SAY "HELLO"?

What is your favorite way of greeting someone? Do you:

HUG

FOR THOSE YOU REALLY CARE ABOUT.
Grandmas love this one best.

WAVE

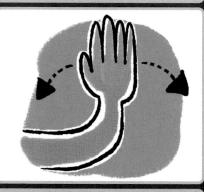

WHEN HUGGING IS TOO AWKWARD.
Good for when you meet new people.

SHAKE HANDS

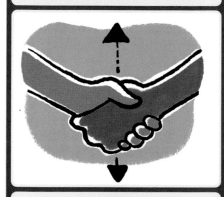

FOR A FORMAL APPROACH.
Watch out for the iron handshake grip!

POUND A FIST BUMP

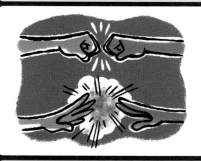

EXPLODE IT FOR EXTRA FLAVOR.
Also try the elbow bump or foot tap, both good alternatives.

GIVE A HIGH FIVE

ALL THE COOL KIDS ARE DOING IT.
Watch out for the super high-fivers—your hands are gonna sting!

DO A SECRET HANDSHAKE

THE ONLY WAY FOR BESTIES!
This one can potentially make other people feel excluded.

You probably know how you like best to say "hello." But before tackling with a hug or releasing a high five with someone, have you asked the other person what they prefer?

Asking first if it's okay to hug, fist bump, or start a synchronized flash-mob dance is called asking for consent. And it's really important to do this, because not everybody is comfortable greeting the same way. In fact, not everybody is comfortable being touched or approached in the same way. So, asking for consent is being respectful of another person's body and level of comfort, or boundaries. When you ask for consent, you create a safe space for everybody. Great job!

Point out your favorite Hello trading card to friends and family and let them know your own boundaries!

PLEASE ASK FIRST

DEALING WITH DILEMMAS

"Oooof! I dropped my toast butter-side down."

"Noooo! My final basketball game is the same day as my best friend's birthday party!"

"Ewww! I stepped in dog poop...again."

What a bunch of problems! But what if handling smaller problems helped you learn how to navigate life? Developing your problem-solving skills now will serve you well for when bigger, grown-up problems might come at you later on. Try it on for size now, and see how you'd solve each of these problems:

WHAT YOU'LL DO

1. You're running really late for school but haven't eaten breakfast yet. What do you do?

_____

_____

_____

2. You're upset because your best friend has decided to play with someone else at recess today. How do you handle it?

_____

_____

_____

3. Your teacher tells everyone to hand in their homework, but—oops!—you forgot yours at home. What do you say?

_____

_____

_____

4. You want to go to your friend's sleepover party, but it's the same night as your sister's school play. How do you deal with it?

_____

_____

_____

5. Your math homework is totally stumping you. How do you get it done?

_____

_____

_____

6. You love playing soccer, but a teammate is bullying you. What can you do?

_____

_____

_____

Think about your answers above. Why did you decide to solve the problems in those ways? Could you have done anything differently?

4 DIFFERENT TYPES OF PROBLEM-SOLVER
WHICH ONE ARE YOU?

"THE FEELER"

When faced with a problem, you always want the best outcome for everyone. Considerate, compassionate, and fair, you put yourself in the other person's shoes in order to find a solution to your dilemma. Your strong values and morals guide you on any challenging path.

"THE LOGIC FAIRY"

For you, problems are like math equations—there's always a logical solution. It's just common sense! You look at all the info, explore every angle in-depth, and leave no stone unturned to figure out the answer to your problem. Your analytical and reasonable brain will get you out of this.

"THE TRUST-YOUR-GUT"

When a problem comes your way, you feel your way out of it. You trust your instincts and don't always worry about facts and information. It's like you have a problem-solving sixth sense, and you use your creativity and imagination to figure things out.

"THE COAXER"

You know what you want and you go after it. No matter what, you always try to get your way, even if that means the other person gets cheated. You might know it's wrong, but problem-solving for you *always* means getting what you want.

ACTION + VISION = ACTIVISM!

Activism is when you take a cause you really care about and do something about it. Kids really do have the power to change the world—no matter how small you may feel, you can do big things.

When you think about the world, what cause do you care most about? It could be climate change, equality for all humans, animal rights…and the list goes on. Identify one cause you really care about and go for it! Take your vision and turn it into action.

WHAT YOU'LL NEED

- Paper
- Markers
- Poster board
- Stickers, magazines, newspapers, and any other decorative items

WHAT YOU'LL DO

1. Write your cause at the top of your paper.

2. Underneath your cause, write some words about why you care about it. These could be single words, phrases, whole sentences, or even pictures. Tap into your feelings! Make it colorful!

3. Underneath those words, write and/or draw pictures about what you want to do about it.

4. And underneath that, put down some more thoughts and pictures about what you *can* do about it.

5. This is your Vision Board. Post it up in your room or school locker so you can always see your thoughts, feelings, and ideas. Whenever you're in doubt about what to do, look to your Vision Board to guide you.

6. Now you're going to design a poster that you'd bring to a protest or rally about your cause. Take out your fresh, blank poster board.

7. Refer to your Vision Board and come up with a few words or a phrase that helps convey your cause to everyone. It can be serious, witty, funny, or honest. This poster will show what the cause means to you and to the world.

8. Write those words in big letters in the middle of your poster board.

9. Around the words, draw pictures that help explain the words. You can even cut out magazines and newspapers to make a collage on your poster.

10. Hang the poster in your room. Then talk to your grown-ups about attending a protest or rally that supports your cause.

Let your voice be heard!

MY SUPERHEROES

Who are your superheroes? Do they save the world, fly up high, and leap buildings in a single bound? Maybe they are people who are important to your community and save lives in a different kind of way.

Your superheroes can be fictional characters you read about or see in the movies. Or they can be real-life, everyday people like your teacher, principal, parents, firefighters, or healthcare workers.

List your superheroes here:

_____

_____

_____

_____

_____

_____

Now list what you admire about your superheroes:

_____

_____

_____

_____

_____

_____

SUPERHERO QUALITIES,™ **RIGHT HERE!**

Could *you* actually be a superhero, disguised as a regular kid? Take a look at all the superhero qualities you listed. Which of these do you also see in yourself? Which of these qualities do you *want* to have?

Whether you already have superhero qualities or are working on getting some, draw YOU as a superhero right here.

Make sure you label all your Superhero Qualities™ on your drawing!

FRIEND OR FRENEMY?

Whether you have tons of friends or just a few—can you tell who's a real friend and who's a frenemy?

REAL FRIENDS are awesome and they make you feel awesome, too. They support you 100 percent and stand up for you in times of trouble.

FRENEMIES are more like foes (or enemies). You know the ones: Sometimes they are really fun to be with, but other times…they make you feel bad about yourself.

How can you tell the difference between real friends and frenemies?

REAL FRIENDS

- You can trust them 100 percent.
- They make you feel safe and supported.
- They cheer you on in whatever you do.
- They give you real advice that is in your best interest.
- You feel super awesome around them.

FRENEMY

- They betray your trust.
- They make you feel wobbly and unsure.
- You have to fake who you are around them.
- They sometimes put you down in front of others.
- They give you advice that is really in their best interest.
- They make you feel less than awesome or even bad about yourself.

MY REAL FRIENDS ARE:

_____
_____
_____

THEY ARE MY REAL FRIENDS BECAUSE:

_____
_____
_____
_____
_____
_____
_____
_____
_____
_____

I RECOGNIZE SOME FRENEMY QUALITIES IN THESE PEOPLE:

_____

_____

_____

THEY MIGHT NOT BE REAL FRIENDS BECAUSE:

_____

_____

_____

_____

_____

_____

_____

_____

_____

_____

Think about the real friends you listed on the previous page. How do they make you feel?

Looking at the answers above, did you notice that some of your friends might actually be frenemies? How do they make you feel about yourself?

If you're hanging out with frenemies and don't want to anymore, what do you think you can do?

Are YOU a real friend?

WHO AM I...
IN THE WORLD?

How do we each find a place to fit in this great, wide world of ours? The world is SO large and complicated; compared to it, we are each so small and simple.

And there are so many people on Earth: about 8 billion! So, how do you figure out who you are in relation to others?

You have a choice about how you present yourself to your family, friends, school, and community, which is great practice for how to place yourself in the world. Who you are is defined both by what you want to be and how others see you.

So, who are YOU in this great, wide world? Try out these experiments to help you find out:

BESTIE QUIZ

Your best friend is someone who allows you to be the true YOU. And you probably bring out their truest self, too. But how well do you *really* know each other?

WHAT YOU'LL NEED

- Your best friend
- Pencil
- Paper (optional)

WHAT YOU'LL DO

1. Down below, answer these quiz questions about yourself. Have your best friend do the same, either in their copy of *The Great Big ME Experiment* or on a sheet of paper. Do *not* show your answers to each other!

2. Then together, ask and answer these quiz questions out loud, but this time answer them about the *other* person.

My favorite color is:

_____

My friend's is:

_____

I hate this food:

_____

My friend hates:

_____

My favorite movie is:

_____

My friend's is:

_____

My favorite TV show is:

_____

My friend's is:

_____

My favorite book is:

_____

My friend's is:

_____

My favorite place in town is:

_____

My friend's is:

_____

My dream pet is:

_____

My friend's is:

_____

My favorite sport is:

_____

My friend's is:

_____

My perfect day is:

_____

My friend's is:

_____

My middle name is:

_____

My friend's is:

_____

My favorite band/song is:

_____

My friend's is:

_____

If I had only one wish it would be:

_____

My friend's would be:

_____

My biggest fear is:

_____

My friend's is:

_____

My favorite food is:

_____

My friend's is:

_____

My favorite candy is:

_____

My friend's is:

_____

My favorite drink is:

_____

My friend's is:

_____

Now compare your answers!

How many answers did you both get correct? Were there any times when your bestie knew more about you...than you?

CUE THE COMPLIMENTS!

Who doesn't like to be complimented? Getting noticed for something nice makes you feel like you're standing on top of this big world. It's cool to know you're appreciated, even for something small and insignificant. Have you ever received a compliment that you still remember to this day?

This experiment will get you to think about the compliments that make you feel good about yourself…and have you start dishing out more compliments to others!

WHAT YOU'LL DO

1. On a piece of paper, write down compliments you remember receiving. They can be recent ones, or others that have stuck in your memory because of how good they made you feel.

2. Now write some compliments you would tell yourself today. They could be anything from "I got a tricky word correct on my spelling quiz" to "I nailed the soccer team tryouts" to "My eyes are really sparkling today." Go all out! Treat yourself to some really nice words.

3. See this big list of compliments here? There might be someone in your life who'd like to hear these kind words, too. Choose your favorite compliment from the list and dole it out to a friend, classmate, or even a random person you encounter in town. Bet you'll get a big smile and enthusiastic "Thanks!"

GENDER WORKSHOP

Now let's take a close look at gender. Have you ever done that before?

Throughout your life, many people have probably told you what your gender is. From the moment you were born, people called you "girl" or "boy." Maybe they had opinions on what you might like or how you should behave because of your gender. Maybe it was assumed you would like certain colors, like pink or blue!

You may also have heard these things said to or about you:

HE IS A TOUGH BOY.

SHE IS A TOMBOY.

SHE IS SUCH A GIRLY GIRL.

HE'S A SENSITIVE BOY.

BOYS SHOULDN'T DO THAT.

GIRLS SHOULDN'T DO THIS.

There are words that are typically used to describe girls and boys:

GIRL

FEMININE   SENSITIVE   DELICATE   NURTURING

EMOTIONAL   PASSIVE   POLITE   HELPFUL

BOY

MASCULINE   TOUGH   POWERFUL   BOLD

ATHLETIC   CONFIDENT   AGGRESSIVE   AMBITIOUS

Have you ever heard any of these words used to describe you? Was it true? Was it false? Have you been told that this is how your gender should behave? How did these words make you feel?

This decision to call you "girl" or "boy" was likely based on your *anatomy*, or your body. If you have a penis, you're usually called "boy." If you have a vulva, you are usually called "girl." But anatomy and gender have nothing to do with each other. Anatomy is science-based, and gender is society-based.

Society has "genderized" certain human qualities, or assigned them to specific genders. But these are *stereotypes*. A stereotype is a general idea of how a person should act, based on what group they might belong to. In this experiment, we are talking about gender stereotypes, or what people think you should act like based on your gender. But human qualities are not for certain genders only. They are for any and all people. What characteristics do you feel describe you best?

You don't have to look and feel the way other people tell you that you should. You are the one who decides how you look to the outside world, and you are the one who knows how you feel inside. The way you look and feel can change from year to year, day to day, and moment to moment

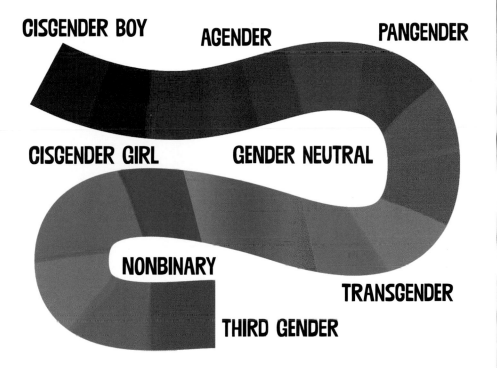

CISGENDER BOY **AGENDER** **PANGENDER**

CISGENDER GIRL **GENDER NEUTRAL**

NONBINARY

TRANSGENDER

THIRD GENDER

You can decide what others should call you: These are known as our pronouns. There are pronouns like:

SHE/HER HE/HIM THEY/THEM ZE/ZIR XE/XEM

And many others, too!

Which of these genders do you identify with?

_____

Which pronouns feel best for you?

_____

Make sure you write in pencil on this page so you can erase and rewrite what you've written at any time.

MY HOUR OF ME

Imagine you had no school, no sports, no chores, and nothing you had to do...for a whole afternoon. If you had a few hours to do whatever you want, what would it be?

MAKE A LIST HERE:

_____
_____
_____
_____
_____
_____
_____
_____

NOW LOOK AT YOUR LIST AND ASK YOURSELF:

- What does my list say about who I am?
- Are the activities on the list all for me? Are any of them for others?
- Are they active or lazy?
- Are they done alone or with others?
- Are any of them dangerous, or am I playing it pretty safe?
- Are there any I've never tried before?
- Is the activity in the top spot the thing I want to do the most?
- Am I able to go and make these things happen?

Is this a WISH LIST or a MUST-DO list?

SAY YES!

In the experiment "Bust Those Habits!" on page 96, you learned how easy it is to get stuck into the same old patterns and routines. Habits are easy and comfortable, and that's what makes us stay trapped there.

When new opportunities come up for you, what do you do? Do you find it easier or more comfortable to say "no"? Or are you a "yes" person?

Tomorrow, try out this experiment: Say "yes" all day long (using your best judgment, of course!), instead of saying "no." When someone asks you a yes/no question, what are you going to answer?

YES, of course!

HERE ARE SOME POSSIBLE SCENARIOS

You walk into the cafeteria and someone new asks you to sit with them for lunch. But you want to sit at your old table of friends like you always do. Say **"yes"** to the new friend, and see if you discover anything interesting from them.

Your band or choir teacher asks you to do the solo in the next school concert. You're usually too shy to stand up by yourself on stage. Say **"yes"** and see what happens!

Your younger sibling needs some help with homework after school. They ask you for help. Say **"yes"** and see if you learn anything while you're being the teacher for a change.

After your day of saying "yes," do you want to say "yes" more often? How did "yes" make you feel? Were you surprised by what you wound up doing? Did you try anything new?

Do you like saying "yes"?

MY HOPE LIST

You've done so many experiments throughout this book to get to know the real YOU. Some of them were probably challenging, and some may have been easy. It's exciting to get to know yourself better, isn't it?

When you know yourself well, you can trust and rely on yourself in good times and bad. This really helps as you begin to grow into an adult.

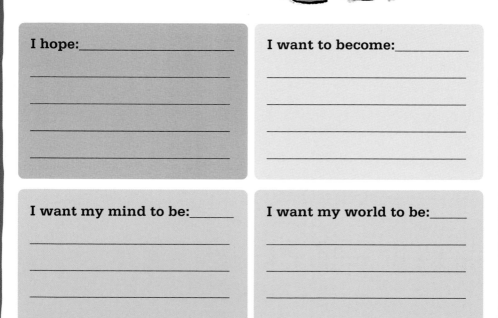

You will change as you grow up, and that's okay. In fact, change is great. Change helps you morph more into the YOU-ness of you.

So, who do you want to be as you change and grow? What world do you envision for your future self? How do you want to shape your mind? What are some of your BIG hopes for the future? List them here:

I hope:_____

_____

_____

_____

_____

I want to become:_____

_____

_____

_____

_____

I want my mind to be:_____

_____

_____

_____

_____

I want my world to be:_____

_____

_____

_____

_____

ACKNOWLEDGMENTS

A GIANT "THANK YOU" goes out to the funnest and most encouraging editor in the entire world, Justin Krasner; primo publisher, Nathalie Le Du; Kat Kopit, Zoe Maffitt, and Starr Baer for cleaning up this book and making this author look goooooood; Christina Quintero and Tae Won Yu for jazzing up this book and making it look super coooooool; and the entire Odd Dot team at Macmillan. I am honored and grateful to be odd alongside you! Daniel Nayeri, I'm so glad our paths crossed on this project, way back when. Thanks for trusting me. Huge thanks to Harry Briggs for making the coolest, wackiest, and funniest pictures for this book.

Claire Easton and Lori Nowicki, my agents at Painted Words, are the biggest champions and cheerleaders a creator could ever hope for. Thanks for long, creative chats, hand-holding when necessary, and general awesomeness.

To my amazing friends and their kids who have let me pick their brains for this book: Leah and Oliver Shoaff, Allyson and Gwen Rosenthal, Claudia and Liberty Heather, and Susan and James Lee—you are the best! Special thanks go to Caroline Carter, PsyD, for vetting "Gender Workshop."

And, I would hardly have figured out who, what, or where I am without my incredible family: Mom, Dad, Tami, Josh, David, Gaye, Lavinia, and Brendan—but most of all, my #1 loves, Alex, Rhys, and Ed.

—Alli

*The experiment on page 128 is based on the Johari Window model, developed by psychologists Joseph Luft and Harrington Ingham in 1955.